Whispers of Grace

An Inspirational Devotional For Daily Encouragement From The Heart Of God

Wendy Anne Hunt

I would like to dedicate this book to my loving husband, and best friend, Kevin. Thank you so much for all of your support.

I love you more with each day that passes, and I am so blessed that God put you in my life.

***

Also, a huge thank you to Kristen Diaz for her absolute labor of love in editing this manuscript! No small task!!

***

And lastly, thank you to the many folks who encouraged me to write this devotional…and thank you for your patience in the waiting!!

Dear Friend,

Whispers of Grace is a daily devotional meant to be read on your knees in a spirit of prayer, quietly resting at the feet of Jesus. As you come before Him each morning, resist the common temptation to rush in and rush out to get on with the business of the day. Rather, stay here in this sweet place of grace and linger. Let Him speak to your heart so tenderly.

I do not remotely think that the content of these daily reflections are in any way comparable to Scripture; they are merely impressions that I believe God has placed upon my heart in order to encourage and refresh His precious children.

This is a book I have been compelled to write. I remember thinking, "I can't keep this to myself; I must share it!" Even now as I read through these pages, I am freshly touched by the Spirit of God, and I feel Him urging me to get this out to His people for the edification and building up of His body.

My passionate desire is to hear and relay through written word the loving heart of God to His beloved children, albeit imperfectly, as we now see through a glass but dimly and hear with fallen ears.

Through the pages of this book, I pray that you who are wearied by the stresses and trials of life will be uplifted and sustained; that you will be brought nearer to our sweet Savior; that you will gain a fresh revelation of His undying love for you and feel the warmth of His loving embrace; that each day you will increasingly savor the richness of His enduring grace toward you; and that you will be encouraged, edified, convicted, exhorted, and challenged in your daily walk with Christ. May each page hold for you a timely word that will speak to your circumstances, and which will be to you as "apples of gold in a setting of silver." (Prov. 25:11)

Amazed by His grace,

Wendy Anne Hunt

"Write the vision; make it plain on tablet, so he may run who reads it." Hab. 2:2

P.S. Not every entry will apply to where you are in your life, but as you read each one, please be thinking about those you love to whom it does apply and feel free to share that entry with them so that God may use it to bless, encourage, and strengthen them.

Some Things You Need To Know Before You Read This Book!

The Bad News

You and I are sinners, and therefore separated from God, who is completely holy.

"For all have sinned and fall short of the glory of God." Rom. 3:23

God, in His justice, punishes sinners.

"For the wages of sin is death…" Rom. 6:23a

We cannot save ourselves in any way.

"All our righteousness and good deeds are as filthy rags." Is. 64:6

The Good News

But, Jesus suffered and died for sinners, in our place, to save us by His grace (free, undeserved gift) through faith in Him.

"…but the gift of God is eternal life in Christ Jesus our Lord." Rom. 6:23b

"But God demonstrates His own love for us in this: While we were still sinners, Christ died for us." Rom. 5:8

YOU can be saved from the penalty of your sins…right now!

"If you confess with your mouth, 'Jesus is Lord,' and believe in your heart that God raised Him from the dead, you will be saved.

For it is with your heart that you believe and are justified (just as if you'd never sinned!), and it is with your mouth that you confess and are saved." Rom. 10:9-10

If you desire put your trust in Christ for the forgiveness of your sins, you can do that right now. Simply pray a prayer something like this from your heart:

Lord, I know that I'm a sinner, and my sin is first and foremost against you. Please forgive me, Lord. I believe that you sent your son, Jesus, to die on the cross in my place, taking all of my sins upon himself, and paying the full penalty for them. Please help me to turn, by the power of your Holy Spirit, from everything that offends you. I place my life and my will into your hands and ask you to be my Lord and Savior all the days of my life.

If you just made a decision to follow Christ, we would love to know about it and to share in your joy, as well as to get some free follow-up materials into your hands that will aid you on this new, glorious journey. Please call:

1-800-NEED-HIM

I hope you enjoy this devotional, and I pray that through its pages you will be encouraged, refreshed, and re-envisioned.

Amazed By His Grace Toward Me,

Wendy Anne Hunt

HuntandPeckPress@gmail.com

www.HuntandPeckPress.com

"As the deer pants for the water brooks, so my soul pants for Thee, O God. My soul thirsts for God, for the living God." Ps. 42:1-2a (NAS)

There are some this morning who would say, "I don't know God like that...I don't yearn for Him; I don't long for Him, my soul doesn't thirst for Him."

But I would say to you this morning that I have known you by name from before the foundation of the earth.

As I hung on the cross 2,000 years ago, do you know whose face I saw?—yours. And I longed for you...I longed to rescue you from your sin and its penalty of death.

I am calling to you this morning, for I have chosen you to be My own precious child.

Will you come to Me now? Will you come and lay your sins at My feet, which were pierced for you, and let Me take the weight and the burden of those sins from you? And if you have already received my free gift of eternal life but have drifted in the closeness of your walk with Me, will you return this day to your first love?

All your life you have thirsted for things that could never quench that thirst. This morning I call you to come and drink and to finally be satisfied.

"'And you will seek Me and find Me when you search for Me with all your heart. And I will be found by you,' declares the Lord." Jer. 29:13-14a (NAS 1977)

Today is the day...will you answer My call and come?

"All of us like sheep have gone astray, each of us has turned to his own way." Isa. 53:6a (NAS)

There are some today who would say, "Yes, that's me. I have wandered, I have strayed, I have turned to my own way."

But listen to My words in Matthew 18:12-13:

"If any man has a hundred sheep, and one of them has gone astray, does he not leave the ninety-nine on the mountains and go and go and search for the one that is straying?

And if it turns out that he finds it, truly I say to you, he rejoices over it more than the ninety-nine which have not gone astray." (NAS)

My dear one, I am the Good Shepherd, and I have left the fold this morning and have ventured into the mountain passes searching for one lost sheep…I am searching for you. Listen in the stillness of your heart, and you will hear that I am calling your name.

Will you let yourself be found by Me, this morning?

"Were not the Ethiopians and the Libyans a huge army with very many chariots and horsemen? Yet, because you relied on the Lord, He gave them into your hand. For the eyes of the Lord run to and fro throughout the whole earth, to give strong support to those whose heart is blameless toward Him." II Chr. 16:8-9a

My child, it is you that My eyes have fallen upon this morning, to **strongly support** you in the battle you are waging in your life right now.

Because you have relied on Me, I will deliver you. Because you have trusted Me in the midst of your difficulties, I will rise up mightily on your behalf.

I will turn the tide of this battle to give you the overwhelming victory because you have not allowed your faith in Me to be shaken. I will hold you up and strengthen your arms.

The battle is great, but your God is greater— mighty, powerful and able to deliver the one who trusts in Him without wavering.

"You did not choose Me, but I chose you." John 15:16

B efore I even created the heavens and the earth, I looked down through the corridors of time, and I saw you…and I loved you, and I chose you to be My very own.

I did not choose you because you were lovely in and of yourself, for I saw even before I created you all the sins you would do that would pierce My heart.

What I saw was the beauty of who you would become in My Son. I saw you righteous, holy, whiter than snow, wholly acceptable and pleasing to Me, the child of My delight.

As this new day begins, remember that you are dearly loved by a Father who gave everything to make you His own precious child.

"And I am sure of this, that He who began a good work in you will bring it to completion [in you until] the day of Christ Jesus." Phil. 1:6

This morning, I give you new hope – I will set My hope in your heart. And that hope will strengthen you and give you courage.

This morning, I give you new vision – Let me renew within you My vision for My church. Let Me also renew within you My vision for your life, My precious child, as you continue to yield your life to Me.

This morning, I place within you a new heart – My heart of mercy and compassion for those who are suffering, that you may be moved to action and be My hands and feet and My arms of comfort to them. Let Me place within you My heart for the lost, for I desire that none should perish! Compel them to come; cry out to them in the streets telling of My love for them, of My blood that was poured out for them, of My burning desire to have a personal relationship with them, of My desire to give them true purpose for their life and to set their hearts free! Compel them to come to Me!

This morning, I give you new joy – Joy in your salvation, and joy in your Savior. And it will bubble up from within you as a spring, an unstoppable fountain, which brings new life and refreshing.

Receive these, My gifts to you, and let the light of My glory shine through you, so that others may be drawn to the flame!

"No soldier in active service entangles himself in the affairs of everyday life, so that he may please the one who enlisted him as a soldier." II Tim. 2:4 (NAS)

My child, free yourself from the entanglement of the things of this world, for they have begun to ensnare you. Shake yourself free from the lustful desire that burns within you for worldly things, for they enemy of your soul seeks to use these to distract you from My purposes and they will only serve to hinder you from following My will with a whole heart and fulfilling the wonderful plans that I have for you.

Submit your desires to Me; lay them at the foot of My cross. For I know all that you have need of.

And in the shadow of the cross, all the unimportant, the unnecessary, the frivolous and lustful desires of your heart all fade away, and your eyes see clearly…your perspective is adjusted and corrected.

For, My child, your desire should be for Me.

Trust Me as your Provider, as your Father, to provide you with all that you need for life and godliness.

One thing I do: Forgetting what lies behind and straining forward to what lies ahead, I press on toward the goal for the prize of the upward call of God in Christ Jesus." Phil. 3:13-14

Are you living a relatively ineffective life for Me, paralyzed spiritually because there are things in your past that are holding you back?

Maybe it is failures, maybe a devastating loss, maybe someone speaking over your life that you will never amount to anything or succeed at that which you try.

But I say to you this morning;

Do not let the past cast a shadow over, and dictate, your future.

Have I called you to a thing?

Then I will give you all the strength and wisdom you need to accomplish it…Have I lit a fire in your soul to do a certain task for My glory – be it humble or great? Then, whether your past would seek to paralyze you with fear of failure and cries of inadequacy or not, I will go before you and make a way. For all things are truly possible when you place your life in My almighty hands!

I choose to use the despised, the rejected, the weak. Know that My plans for you are good, and I can and will accomplish them in My power!

Now as they went on their way, Jesus entered a village. And a woman named Martha welcomed Him into her house. And she had a sister called Mary, who sat at the Lord's feet and listened to His teaching. But Martha was distracted with much serving. And she went up to Him and said, 'Lord, do you not care that my sister has left me to serve alone? Tell her then to help me.' But the Lord answered her, 'Martha, Martha, you are anxious and troubled about many things, but one thing is necessary. Mary has chosen the good portion, which will not be taken away from her.'" Luke 10:38-42

My child, you are distracted by so many, many things in your life…even some good things that have caused you to lose focus.

But really only one thing is necessary…that you come and sit at My feet, listen to My words, and let them resound in your heart, and let Me shower My love on you.

Quiet and still your heart and mind. Don't rush in and rush out of your times with Me. Stay here, linger here, and feel your strength renewing.

Out of the strength, vision, and peace that you receive here from Me will flow all else that matters.

"For [the Lord] is good, For His steadfast love endures forever." II Chr. 5:13b

My child, tenderly I speak to you this morning...I love you.

You readily receive these words for everyone else, but struggle to hear that it is to you that I speak. This morning I would speak to your heart these words once again...I love you. I withheld nothing from you—not even My very life.

Receive these words, not for the person next to you, not for your spouse or children, not as a general proclamation to the church as a whole, but for you.

Let these words sink deeply into your spirit; let them find their target upon your heart and make their mark upon your life...I love you!

When you truly hear these words, not with your ears, but with your heart, you will never be the same again...you cannot. So hear them once again this morning, or maybe actually hear them for the first time, these sweet words of grace...let them go down to your innermost being and satisfy as the choicest of morsels...

I love you!

My child, are you in love with Me this morning? Am I the One who has captivated your soul and captured your heart? Just as an earthly lover, does your heart beat faster when you get a glimpse of Me? When life gets busy and cares come pressing in, do you seek for My face in the crowd?

As you fall deeper in love with Me, your Savior and Lord, your Husband, your Friend...as you fall deeper in love with Me, you will find obedience will become a joyful pleasure rather than a struggle. It will no longer be submitting to a law or a standard, but rather pleasing the heart of your Friend, pleasing the heart of your Beloved. You will find that the guilt and self-condemnation of failure will give way to gratefulness and joy, for you will know the heart of Him whom you strive to please, that it is tender toward you and forgiving, and that it rejoices in your efforts as well as in your successes.

Come, My love, and walk with Me in the cool of the garden this morning. Let your heart fall in love with Me this day. Then obey Me because you love Me, and sweet and productive will be your labors.

W hen we willfully walk into sin, thereby placing ourselves under the heavy hand of God the Father's discipline, it's not like He's 'out to get us'...rather, He's 'out to get us back'!

"Therefore, confess your sins to each other and pray for each other so that you may be healed. The prayer of a righteous person is powerful and effective." Jas. 5:16 (NIV)

"If we confess our sins, He is faithful and just and will forgive us our sins and purify us from all unrighteousness." I John 1:9 (NIV)

"And looking upon them Jesus said to them, 'With man this is impossible, but with God all things are possible.'" Matt. 19:26

There are some this morning who are facing what seems like an impossible situation or circumstance in their lives…like a dark mountain looming large before you, one you can find no path around, a treacherous mountain that you cannot climb over, overwhelming and insurmountable.

But I would ask you, My child, is **anything** too difficult for Me? Remember your impossible plight when you were dead in your sin and so desperately in need of a Savior to cleanse and forgive you, to breathe new life into you, and to present you reconciled to the Father holy and blameless? It was impossible with man, but not impossible through My blood shed for you.

Look to the cross, and remember how I met your **greatest** and most **impossible** need there. And from there gather strength, courage, and hope. For if I did not hold back My very blood from you but rather let it flow freely to rescue you, will I not even now rush to the aid of My beloved one?

Nothing is impossible for Me!

O My children, just rest here in the presence of your Savior. Don't **strive**… just **be** with Me. I did **all** the work on the cross so that you would not have to work your way into My presence…you can just freely come and receive, for by My blood you are completely clean and made wholly worthy. Because you have been washed in My blood, I have declared you perfect in My eyes, righteous, pure.

Completely cleansed, made totally free,
There is no stain at all upon thee;
Nailed to the cross, your debt fully paid,
Now freely come and receive of Me!

"The heavens are telling of the glory of God, and their expanse is declaring the work of His hands." Ps. 19:1 (NAS)

My child, the evidence is resounding—the sun, moon, and stars, every sunrise and sunset, every child born, every creature with the breath of life, the amazing details of the human body, every atom and molecule, the unique and intricate design of every snowflake—all trumpet forth My existence, My power, My majesty!

Yet, though the eyes and hearts of many are darkened to these obvious truths, to **you** I have revealed My glory.

Now, you have this treasure in earthen vessels. And what is this treasure? It is the revelation of Christ, crucified for you and raised to give you new life! It is the glory of the cross of His grace toward you!

Oh joy, My children, for I have made known to you the things that cause even the angels to marvel and stand in awe of Me!

And why to **you** when so many others continue in darkness? Rejoice in My love for you this day…that I have moved heaven and earth to make **you** mine!

Desire Me

"The eyes of all mankind look up to You for help; You give them their food as they need it. You constantly satisfy the hunger and thirst of every living thing. (The Lord) is close to all who call upon Him sincerely. He fulfills the desires of those who reverence and trust Him." Ps. 145:15-16, 18

Hunger after Me, and you will be filled to overflowing. Thirst for Me, and I will quench your thirst with cool, refreshing water. Desire Me, and you will not be found wanting, for I will fill you with Myself and satisfy your soul.

Do not look for another to bring you joy, contentment, and fulfillment. Do not look for a thing to bring happiness to your soul. You will know contentment only in My presence. You will know true joy and peace only as you sit at My feet.

"I will rejoice greatly in the Lord, my soul will exult in my God; for He has clothed me with garments of salvation, He has wrapped me with a robe of righteousness, as a bridegroom decks himself with a garland, and as a bride adorns herself with her jewels." Isa. 61:10 (NAS)

My child, come and let Me clothe you this morning, for once again you have cast off My robes of righteousness and you walk about naked and ashamed. You have allowed guilt to cast its black and paralyzing shadow over you once more.

But I call you to remember how sweet is the freedom of My forgiveness and grace. Remember the joy that filled your heart when you realized that I paid it **all**, that I covered you **completely** with **My** holiness and **My** righteousness, that I washed you whiter than the driven snow, and that now there was, and **never would be, any** stain upon you, for it was **finished** once and for all—

You are clean!

Come now, and let me clothe you once again in these priceless, precious garments, and walk once more in My freedom and joy!

"For the eyes of the Lord are on the righteous, and His ears are open to their prayer." I Pet. 3:12

If My eye is on the sparrow, how much more is My eye upon My little children whom I have birthed into life?

Will I not care for you, My little child? Does not My merciful Father's heart hear every time you cry to Me for help? Do not tears form in My eyes each time I see them fall from yours?

But I, My little child, see the end from the beginning, and I am filled with hope for your future, for I am already there...And I already have a plan, and have from eternity past prepared this way that you should walk in it. Although you cannot see the way clearly right now, I ask you to follow Me, your Shepherd and Guide, as I light the path before you.

For in the day in which things seem well, I will be a cloud for you to follow in My ways. And in the night, when the darkness seems to overcome you, I will shine all the brighter as a pillar of fire and will lead you safely in the pathway of righteousness...

You can trust Me with your life...

You can **trust** Me with your life...

Come away with Me, My love

Draw away with Me into the light of My presence, the place where I can refresh your spirit and restore your soul as you bask in My wondrous love and acceptance.

And I will lift your countenance, and your heart will once again be filled with song. And you will sing there as in the days of your youth, as in the days when I first called you by your name.

You will run once again as a child splashing in the streams of My love, dancing through vast open fields, and you will laugh easily and freely, with joyous laughter and with wholehearted delight, for I will set your spirit free, My child. I will turn your sorrow into dancing, and O what incredible joy will overflow your soul.

So come, My love—draw close to Me, and then draw closer still...and I will refresh you and restore the youthful and childlike joy of your heart.

I will set your spirit free!

Draw close to Me and I will draw close to you.

I desire to be with you and to pour Myself upon you…to shower you with My love, My precious daughter, My precious son.

Come…My presence brings rest and great refreshing. Like cool rain falling on your spirit on a hot summer's day, I will pour My rain upon all your dry places. And you will know new and abundant growth and life as you draw near.

So come and rest here in My presence. Yes come, all you who are weary and heavy laden and I will give you rest. For I will care for you, and I will surely accomplish all that concerns you.

Come, unload every burden you bear and allow Me to take them, and in exchange receive the rest and refreshing of being with Me.

"[And they made an oath to the Lord] with their whole heart and had sought Him earnestly, and He let them find Him. So the Lord gave them rest on every side." II Chr. 15:15 (NAS)

Rejoice!

Rejoice in Me, My child...Yes, shout aloud with great joy unto your Faithful God and the One who is able to deliver you!

Do not look to the circumstances around you; rather, look to My faithfulness. I have told you that in the world you will have tribulation, but take courage; I have overcome the world.

My child, focus not so much on the trial as on Me and My ability to bring you through it. Do not allow despair to settle in your heart as you are overwhelmed by the circumstances that surround you and hem you in on every side. Do not fear when the deep waters seem to swallow you up; rather, rejoice in Me.

Praise Me unceasingly for My great faithfulness in the course of your life. Is this trial any different than the many others I have brought you through? I am a faithful God. I am true to My Word. I will surely see you through to the other side.

So rejoice and be light in heart, knowing this: I, your Deliverer, see and know and have already made a way!

"Do not lean on your own understanding. In all your ways acknowledge Him and He will make your paths straight." Prov. 3:5-6 (NAS)

"Therefore we do not lose heart, but though our outer man is decaying yet our inner man is being renewed day by day. And these light and momentary trials are producing for us an eternal weight of glory far beyond all comparison." II Cor. 4:16-17 (NAS)

Are you overwhelmed by various physical challenges you are facing? Have you forgotten, My child...you are not home yet. This is not your final destination. You are a traveler passing through this broken down, decaying world on your way to your glorious home with Me.

There sickness, disease, decay, pain, fear, sorrow will be no more.

Set your eyes on the glory that is to come, and you will find hope and the strength to endure today.

"...If you abide in Me and I abide in you, you will bear much fruit..." John 15:5

"Use me, Lord," you say. Yet you strive to do these works in your **own** strength instead of mine. The abiding must come first, and then the labor. You must linger in the nearness of Me. You must breathe in the sweet fragrance of the presence of your Lord. You must come and allow My life-giving Spirit to wash over your soul and change you from glory to glory...**then** I will use you. And the fruit that you bear will remain; it will be sweet and choice fruit, and all who enjoy it will give glory to the Most High God!

"This is My commandment, that you love one another, just as I have loved you." John 15:12 (NAS)

My children, where there are poor and needy among you, I call you to help them bear their crosses; I call you to do all the good you can for them; I call you to meet their needs to the best of your ability.

Where there are weak, doubting, tempted, and comfortless among you, I call you to plead for them daily in prayer, and to walk alongside and help them when their strength fails.

Where there are new believers and babes among you, I call you to be eager to help them mature, teaching them all that I have, in My grace, taught you.

Cease living for yourself, My children, and look to serve My beloved ones. For in blessing others, you will be truly blessed yourself!

My little children, My heart is tender and full of love for you this morning. Though you stumble, I will not condemn you. Rather, My desire is to pick you up, to strengthen and help you, if you will simply reach out and take My outstretched hand.

For haven't I told you in My word that I am compassionate and gracious, slow to anger, and abounding in lovingkindness? That is who I am.

And I who formed you know your frame, My child, that you are but dust. I know the weaknesses that you struggle with and the sins which so easily beset you. I will give you the strength that you need to stand, if you will just take My hand.

"For this is what the Sovereign Lord says: 'I Myself will search for My sheep and look after them. As a Shepherd looks after His scattered flock when He is with them, so will I look after My sheep. I will rescue them from all the places where they were scattered on a day of clouds and darkness…I will search for the lost and bring back the strays. I will bind up the injured and strengthen the weak…'" Ezek. 34:11-12, 16a (NIV)

My child, what things have stolen your affections from Me? What idols have you erected between us that are holding you back from coming and following Me with all your heart?

I plead with you…tear them down! Tear them down before they fall on you and crush you...and, although it seems an impossible task because you well see the great strength and fortitude of them, I will help you. For what is impossible with men is possible with God.

And know this...that nothing you give up for My glory will go without reward. I will give you greater treasures than these, and in great abundance will I give to you.

Y ou have been away too long, My child.

You've been away from My presence much too long. Your own condemnation has driven you far from My courts and continues to keep you away.

But just as the Father, when the prodigal son returned, ran to his unfaithful son, put upon him the best robe, put a ring upon his hand and sandals on his feet, killed the fatted calf and said "Let us eat and be merry, for my son has returned," even so do I, your heavenly Father, rejoice greatly when you once again turn your heart toward Me and come to Me.

"…The Lord, the Lord God, compassionate and gracious, slow to anger, and abounding in lovingkindness and truth; who keeps lovingkindness for thousands, who forgives iniquity, transgression and sin..." Exod. 34:6-7a (NAS)

"Let the word of Christ dwell in you richly." Col. 3:16

Picture with me, My child, an emaciated man, eyes sunken in, flesh hanging loosely from his boney frame, sitting at a banquet table full of exquisite food, yet refusing to nourish himself with the plenty set before him.

My child, you are that man…you are slowly, gradually starving yourself to death.

This world is sapping the very life out of you and robbing you of every ounce of strength.

My word is meat for your soul and nourishment to your bones. But, you are denying yourself the very sustenance that you need. I have prepared a table before you, but you keep pushing the plate away.

Such abundance, such bounty, have I placed before you. There is an ample amount at My table for you to feast, and also to have a nourishing word to strengthen others who are weak and failing. But how will you strengthen others if you yourself are weak and ailing?

Strengthen yourself at My table of delights this morning by feasting on My word.

"God opposes the proud, but gives grace to the humble." Jas. 4:6

O My people, come to Me with a contrite heart. Approach Me with a humble spirit. And I will hear your cry and will heal you and will restore you unto Myself. For a tender heart and a humble spirit I will not despise, but rather I will show Myself strong on your behalf. For I set My hand in opposition against the proud and lofty. But if you will come to Me with a humble and broken spirit, I will pour out lavishly My grace and favor upon you and will draw you unto Myself. Come My precious child. Come My lovely bride in whom is all My delight. Come My little lamb to the arms of your Shepherd...

Come with a humble heart and I will draw you near to Me.

There are so many things that clatter and clamor for your attention and your affection, My child. But I am not in the storm; I am not in the fire...Mine is a still, small voice.

Come and listen—incline your ear—for it is as you come unto Me, basking in the light of My presence and listening to My still, small voice, that I can bring you the true comfort and peace that you so long for.

I love you, My child. I have called you by name, and you are Mine.

I have prepared for you from the beginning of time good works that you should walk in, in order to bring glory to My Name and to reflect Christ to a dying world.

But right now, My child, you are too focused on yourself, on your own needs, on gratifying the lusts and desires of your flesh.

You must put your focus back on Me. Make me your Lord once again and not only your Savior. Turn over every aspect of your life to Me.

For the time is short, and great is the darkness of the days, but how brightly I can shine through a heart submitted and yielded to My will.

So, again I say, put your focus back on Me, My love, and walk joyfully in the good works that I have prepared for you to do in My Name that you may glorify your Father in heaven, and that many will be drawn unto salvation before My soon-coming return!

I have made you for Myself, and you are the work of My hands. I didn't simply allow you to exist; I am the One who formed you and knit you together in your mother's womb.

And, not only did I make you, but I chose you before the foundation of the world. When My eyes saw your unformed substance, I smiled and said, This one's Mine!

Then, when as yet your heart was far from Me and your sins were rising up as an offense before Me, I died in your place so that you could be My child—just as I had predestined you to be—and so that I could draw you near and you could call Me "Father."

My hand has been upon you from the time I formed you. Would you now question My goodness and plans for your future? Would you lack faith for the days to come? Have I not declared that I have written all of the days that were formed for you, when as yet there were none of them? Look at the rich history of My hand upon your life, and there draw strength and faith for future grace.

C ome to Me and listen, for one word from Me can change the course of a nation, one word from Me can change the course of your life.

Come to Me and listen; you ask for wisdom, but in your flurry to try to find it you miss My whisper that seeks to give it.

Come to Me and listen, for though you listen to many other voices, My voice alone can bring sweet peace; Mine alone can inspire you—refresh you; Mine alone can awaken you, ignite your soul; Mine alone can comfort you, strengthen you, sustain you; Mine alone can breathe new life into your spirit; and Mine alone can fill your heart with vibrant, unspeakable joy!

Come to Me and listen, for the world is screaming out to you, trying to capture your attention, and your affections. But I wish to speak softly to you of My undying, never-ending, never-changing, never-failing, tender love. My beloved one, My bride, come and still your heart and mind, and listen to the voice of your Bridegroom.

"And Mary said: 'My soul glorifies the Lord, and my spirit rejoices in God my Savior… For the Mighty One has done great things for me—holy is His Name!'" Luke 1:46-47, 49 (NIV)

Are you focused on your difficulties, circumstances, and trials this morning, or on the many, many reasons you have to rejoice in Me; on all the things that are left undone, or on the many great things I have already accomplished and am continuing to accomplish for you, in you, and through you; on your shortcomings and weaknesses, or on My abundant mercies, which are new for you every single morning you wake?

Like Mary, let your soul exult in Me this day, and let your spirit rejoice in the loving God who, in His mercy and kindness, has saved you…For truly I have done great things for you!

D on't believe what your heart would say about you; don't believe what your mind would reason about you; instead, believe what I say about you in My Word.

Hear My Spirit speak softly to your heart of hearts of My unfailing devotion and faithfulness. Does the opinion of any other really matter to you? I love you deeply with an undying love.

I have never left you, even in the times of your unfaithfulness to Me. Oh, I have wept for you; I have cried out on your behalf; but I have never, ever left you, and I never, ever will. I love you, My precious child.

"...because God has said, 'Never will I leave you; never will I forsake you.'" Heb. 13:5b (NIV)
"Therefore, brothers, since we have confidence to enter the holy places by the blood of Jesus...and since we have a great Priest over the house of God, Let us draw near with a true heart in full assurance of faith, with our hearts sprinkled clean from a [guilty] conscience." Heb. 10:19-22

O My beloved, do not shrink back this morning. Do not allow Satan to cripple you and make you ineffective by weighing you down with a guilty conscience. For I have sprinkled your heart clean from a guilty conscience, and what I have made clean, let no man call unclean.

Let the enemy of your soul not gain victory over you by placing a heavy burden of condemnation upon you. For there is therefore now no condemnation for those who have put their trust in Me. I died to take your sin and its condemnation upon Myself. I cleansed you with My blood and made you **completely** clean. I set you **totally free** from sin's **power** and **guilt.**

Rejoice this morning, for "How blessed is he whose transgression is forgiven, whose sin is covered!" Ps. 32:1

Your problems **seem** great, My child. But I am greater. You feel overwhelmed by the weight of your pressures and concerns, but I tell you to cast all of your cares upon Me and to trust Me with them. My child, I call you today to look at your situation in light of My many attributes. You are powerless, but I am all-powerful. You are confused and perplexed, but I have all knowledge -- I know the beginning from the end, and I have all things under My control. You are so small, frail, and finite, but I am not limited by anything...not by time or space, not by financial constraints, not by anything.

In your finite mind you try to figure out where your help and your deliverance will come from and what form it will take. I tell you that I have ways that you know not of and I will do it. I will do it in a way that you are not anticipating, so that you will know that it was My hand that brought this to you, and so that you may glorify Me.

May your heart be still and your mind not be troubled.

For remember that I am your loving Father who has your best interests at heart, and I will do this thing.

"Do not let your heart be troubled, neither let it be fearful."
John 14:27b (NAS)

"Seek the Lord while He may be found; Call upon Him while He is near. Let the wicked forsake his way and the unrighteous man his thoughts. Let him return to the Lord, that He may have compassion on him, and to our God, for He will abundantly pardon." Isa. 55:6-7

Yes, My child, I **will** abundantly pardon. For this is My heart toward you...grace, mercy, and forgiveness.

What sin consumes your thoughts right now and looms before your guilty conscience? I knew about that sin as I hung on the cross for you, and I covered it there with My blood.

Don't you know that before the world began I saw your sin, but I had a plan to save you from it, draw you to Myself, and call you My own?

I will hold you by the hand, and I will help you to stand so that your foot will not stumble.

"I have swept away your offenses like a cloud, Your sins like the morning mist. Return to Me, for I have redeemed you!" Isa. 44:22 (NIV)

"I will not fail you or forsake you...Only be strong and very courageous. Be careful to do according to all the law which Moses My servant commanded you; Do not turn from it to the right or to the left...Have I not commanded you? Be strong and courageous! Do not tremble or be dismayed, for the Lord your God is with you wherever you go." Josh. 1:5b-9 (NAS)

Yes, be strong and courageous, for I offer you hope and a bright future this morning. Your unforeseen circumstances were not unforeseen to Me...they did not surprise Me. They do not change My precious promises to you. My promises to you are not based on your circumstances or how you feel. My promises are Yes! And Amen! And they **stand firm!**

I **will** be **with** you wherever you go!

I say again, be strong and very courageous! Trust in Me; trust in the word I have spoken to you.

"'For I know the plans I have for you,' says the Lord. 'They are plans for good and not for disaster, to give you a future and a hope.'" Jer. 29:11 (NLT)
"I would have despaired unless I had believed that I would see the goodness of the Lord in the land of the living." Ps.27:13 (NAS)

My child, do you believe that I have **good** for **you? Good** for **your** life? You encourage others often in this, but do you believe it for yourself, or do doubts of My goodness cast a shadow over your thoughts of Me? Fear of failure, fear of lack of provision, fear that the help you are crying out to Me for will not come?

Yes, right now there are difficulties. But why would you interpret that to indicate that I am not **for** you but **against** you?

Look back upon the many times I have brought good from evil in your life, joy from pain, triumph from tragedy, victory from difficulties and trials.

When all seems against you, never doubt that I am **for** you and that I have **good** for you.

"Come to Me, all who are weary and heavy-laden, and I will give you rest." Matt. 11:28 (NAS)

My dear child, there is rest…there is refreshment…in My sweet presence.

Don't make some mere mental ascent, but rather come **fully** and **completely** before Me this morning…Come into My presence, and engage your heart with Me even now.

For I long to be with you…to speak tenderly to you, to encourage your heart…to share glorious and wonderful things with you.

For I am the Lover of your soul, and you are Mine. And O how I **long** for the desire of **your** heart to be for **Me!**

Come and be filled with the joy that only comes from being with Me. Let the joy of My presence refresh and strengthen you. Let it carry you and sustain you when you are weary.

Come and let Me **satisfy** you with My goodness!

"Praise the Lord! Oh give thanks to the Lord, for He is good; for His lovingkindness is everlasting." Ps. 106:1 (NAS)

My child, I know that things are hard right now. Your cries have not gone unheard.

But this morning, I would gently and lovingly challenge you – will you rejoice, even in the dark; and will you praise and thank Me, even when the world would look on and say you have no reason to?

It's a choice to rejoice, but you must trust in My goodness when things are darkest.

I **am** good, and I **have** good for **you**. You must choose to praise when you can't see around the mountain before you. Will you trust that I will work even **this** for your **good**?

When you can't change your circumstances, you **can** change your heart with the help of My Spirit.

Let your trust and faith in My goodness bring hope to your heart and a song of praise from your lips.

Walk On

"I am He who will sustain you. I have made you and I will carry you; I will sustain you and rescue you." Isa. 46:4 (NIV) "How blessed is the man whose strength is in You, in whose heart are the highways to Zion. Passing through the Valley of Baca [weeping] they make it a spring; the early rain also covers it with blessings. They go from strength to strength." Ps. 84:5-7a (NAS)

Some this morning are going through this "valley of weeping," this dry and barren wasteland that seems unable to sustain any life…so desolate, so seemingly purposeless.

But My child, My word to you this morning is "Walk on"…set your face as a flint, your unbroken gaze upon Me, and walk on…not in your own strength or you will stumble.

Rather, walk on in My strength. And as you go you will watch in amazement as I transform the very landscape of this place before you. Instead of bitter tears, it will become a place of springs, covered with pools of life-giving, refreshing water. My arms will comfort you, My grace sustain you, and I will restore joy to your soul once more and cause your heart to sing My praises. You will go from strength to strength, and I will surely lead you safely to the other side in My time.

You will reach back and take hold of the hands of those who come behind you, who find themselves in this place of desolation. And I will use you to guide them, that from your journey you may teach others to sing songs of praise in the darkest of nights.

By the light of your life you will lead others through this valley, and by your steadfastness you will steady the steps of those who falter, that they, too, might "walk on" and go from strength to strength.

In the first part of Hosea 2, God describes and condemns Israel's blatant unfaithfulness to Him, how they had turned away and rejected Him.

But, starting in verse 14, God describes His beautiful and tender plan to restore her, speaking kindly to her and drawing her back to Himself as His bride.

What love, what kindness, what mercy, what grace, what compassion, what forgiveness, what hope we find at the foot of the cross!

Would you describe yourself as faithless…meaning without faith?

Would you consider yourself unfaithful?

Maybe you've fallen…and fallen hard. Maybe you have even, like Peter, denied Him vehemently.

I believe that God would say to you this morning:

My dear one, I will restore you, this moment, if you will simply turn and place your hand in Mine. I died for your unfaithfulness, to cover it with My blood, to wash it away, to forgive it.

I am rich in mercy, and My love for you has never, ever lessened, and never, ever will…even when you are unfaithful to Me.

I love you, My child…return to Me…return to Me, for I wait with outstretched arms for you.

My little one, when you look to your future, what do you see? Do you see the brightness of My glory, or do you see a dark cloud of fear and uncertainty? What rises in your heart when you look at the days to come…the hope of heaven or utter despair?

This morning, I would call you to lift your eyes from the temporal and place them on the eternal. Lift your eyes from the earthly and set them upon the heavenly. What a great hope you have in Me. I have not only forgiven you and set you free; I have gone to prepare a place for you, a wonderful place, that where I am there you may also be!

Let hope, glorious hope, fill your hearts and minds this morning. I will come again; I will return for you, My Bride, and you will live with Me forever in this place where there are no more tears, no more sorrow, no more sickness, no more death. Rejoice! Rejoice! And let hope rise once again in your heart!

"Why are you cast down, O my soul, and why are you in turmoil within me? Hope in God; for I shall again praise him, my salvation and my God"! Ps. 42:11

My beloved one, why do you mourn as a wife forsaken or bereaved?...for I have not abandoned you, and I never will. Why do you weep as an orphan child left utterly alone and with no hope?...for I will never leave you alone but will always remain faithfully by your side. And you are never without hope, because I am your hope. And, My dear one, why do you flog yourself as a prisoner guilty and condemned to death?...for have I not taken all of your punishment upon Myself and replaced it with My grace, mercy, and righteousness?

Let your heart hold fast to these truths. Bind them on; remind yourself of them often. Teach them to your children as you walk along the way.

D raw near to Me, and I will draw near to you! And in My tender presence you will find renewed strength where your strength has waned. You will find renewed hope where you had been overwhelmed by life's cares. You will find renewed faith where faith had been lacking. You will find renewed peace for your restless soul. And you will find renewed joy to lift your heavy heart. Draw near to Me in the sweetness of My presence, and I will draw near to you.

O, My dear child, do not doubt for one moment My tender and undying love for you. O the pain that it causes My heart when you do this. For I sent My only Son to die in your place, which proves My love for you.

Dear child, don't negate and make worthless the costly sacrifice I paid by listening to the lies of the enemy telling you that I don't care for you! Don't make it a cheap, casual offering, for it cost Me everything to ransom you back--and it was all because of My deep, fathomless, tender love for you.

Don't ever doubt, but only look to the cross and hear Me say,

I love you, My child... I love you this much!

"For I consider that the sufferings of this present time are not worthy to be compared with the glory that is to be revealed to us. For the anxious longing of the creation waits eagerly for the revealing of the sons of God...
...For we know that the whole creation groans and suffers the pains of childbirth together until now. And not only this, but also we ourselves, having the first fruits of the Spirit, even we ourselves groan within ourselves, waiting eagerly for our adoption as sons, the redemption of our body. For in hope we have been saved...with perseverance we wait eagerly for it."
Rom. 8:18-19, 22-25 (NAS)

My child, what do you hope for? What is the anxious longing of your heart? What do you wait eagerly for? Do you long for the things this world has to offer -- the fleeting, temporal rewards of a fallen world?

My child, may you look to Me and long for My appearing and for your adoption as My son as much as I am anxiously waiting and longing to come again and take you as My own. May your heart be filled with the anticipation of that great day when I will come for you...and I will come, My child. I will come for you! Wait eagerly, with great hope and anticipation for My return!

"Ho! Everyone who thirsts, come to the waters; and you who have no money come buy and eat. Come buy wine and milk without money and without cost. Why do you spend money for what is not bread, and your wages for what does not satisfy? Listen carefully to Me and eat what is good, and delight yourself in abundance." Isa. 55:1-3a (NAS)

My child, you hunger. But you have been hungering after the wrong things. You eat, but are never satisfied, because you are not eating of the rich, sustaining, nourishing food that I provide.

My child, you thirst. But you have been drinking from the wrong wells. You drink, but your thirst is never quenched, and you are left wanting.

But I would say to you this morning that I am the Bread of Life. My words are food for your soul. I am the Living Water of which you will drink and **never thirst again!**

Come to My table this morning, for I have provided you a rich feast of delights to **truly** satisfy as nothing in this world that you have been seeking can; to nourish, to sustain, to bring life and health and peace, to give you strength—strength to run the race before you—strength to **finish well!**

Come to My table, and partake this morning, and be **truly** satisfied.

"And it came about that as He was approaching Jericho, a certain blind man was sitting by the road, begging. Now hearing a multitude going by, he began to inquire what this might be. And they told him that Jesus of Nazareth was passing by. And he called out, saying, 'Jesus, Son of David, have mercy on me!' And those who led the way were sternly telling him to be quiet; but he kept crying out all the more, 'Son of David, have mercy on me!'" Luke 18:35-38 (NAS 1977)

There are many, so many blind sitting along the roadside today. But I am looking, I am waiting, for the one who would turn and look to Me and cry out from the bottom of his heart, "Jesus, Son of David, have mercy on me, a sinner!" O, cry out to Me today...seek Me while I may be found; call upon Me while I am near. O sinner, forsake your evil ways and thoughts, and cry out to Me, and I will have compassion on you and will abundantly pardon. Cry out to Me today from the depths of your being, **"Jesus, Son of David, have mercy on me!"**

The book of Ezra tells us about the temple of the Lord. It was glorious and magnificent, beautiful and majestic. The Spirit of the Lord filled His temple with the glory of God.

It then speaks of the destruction of that temple-- how it was pillaged and plundered and devastated by the enemy. But then God brought back some of those who were taken into captivity to rebuild His temple and once again make it a glorious place where His glory could dwell.

Each of us is a temple of the most high God.

But some of us, once glorious and magnificent, have allowed ourselves to be pillaged and plundered, devastated by the enemy of our souls. But I believe God is saying to you:

I am bringing you out of your captivity -- come out!--for it is time to rebuild! Build Me a temple, a place where My glory and power can dwell. Rebuild the walls; rebuild the altar of worship; rebuild the temple of your hearts.

"Arise and shine, for your light has come, and the glory of the Lord is risen upon you!" (Isaiah 60:1).

"And there is no creature hidden from His sight, but all things are open and laid bare to the eyes of Him with whom we have to do.
Since then we have a great High Priest who has passed through the heavens, Jesus the Son of God, let us hold fast our confession.
For we do not have a High Priest who cannot sympathize with our weaknesses, but one who has been tempted in all things as we are, yet without sin.
Let us therefore draw near with confidence to the throne of grace, that we may receive mercy and may find grace to help in time of need." Heb. 4:13-16(NAS)

My precious child, do not let the enemy of your soul lie to you that you are forsaken; that you have been abandoned by Me; that I am indifferent to your struggles, sufferings, and pain; that I don't care what you are going through.

For I have seen your tears in the night. Your cries have risen to My ears. I care more deeply than you can even imagine. My child, you are My little one, in whom is all My delight, and it breaks My heart to see you suffer so.

But know this—that I have already made provision for you to come through to the other side of this victorious, if you will appropriate My mercy, grace, and strength. They are here for you, freely available and abundant.

Draw near with confidence to My throne of grace. Take hold of these My gifts to you—mercy, grace to help, courage, comfort, divine strength, and hope.

My child, why do you shrink back as if I am a cruel father or a harsh taskmaster?

Cast your gaze upon Me, and let the love you see in My eyes for you melt away any inhibitions, fear, or condemnation you may have and usher you into My presence.

Come with great joy—holding nothing back—knowing that you are accepted, forgiven, adopted, and beloved by Me.

Like a child running into the arms of the father he knows loves him unconditionally, here I stand extending My opened arms to you without condition. Run into My waiting embrace, beloved.

Then sit quietly at My feet, in the peace of My presence. In the stillness, behold My countenance and be refreshed by it. And I will pour into you of My Spirit and fill you to overflowing. Then you will be a powerful light to this world as the overflow of My love spills out on all those whose lives you touch!

My child, this morning I would remind you of My undying, never-ending love for you.

But your heart cries out 'Unworthy! Unfaithful!', and so you have been.

But God…

"But God, being rich in mercy, because of His great love with which He loved us, even when we were dead in our transgressions and sin, made us alive together with Christ (by grace you have been saved)." Eph. 2:4

My child, let these words reassure your heart—for it is not about you and what you've done; but it is **all** about **Me** and what I've done.

For by My **grace I saved** you, By My **grace** I'll **keep** you, And by My **grace** I will bring you home and present you as My Bride, without blemish or wrinkle, wrapped in My white, spotless robe of righteousness, the delight of My eyes and the joy of My heart!

My amazing grace **bought** you when you were dead in your sin and My enemy.

My amazing grace will **keep you** in Me and is able to keep you from stumbling And My amazing grace will bring you to glory and present you blameless before the Father, made perfect in **My** perfection, made worthy by **My** worthiness, made **completely** clean and holy by the washing of My blood.

Rejoice this morning in My amazing grace toward you!!

B eside the streams of quiet, peaceful waters...this is where I lead you. I will guide you to the greener, richer pastures if you will but follow Me. Though My way is not always easy, it is always the best way.

Though the road by which I lead you to streams and pastures may be rocky and mountainous, on the other side there is rest and peace, joy and great abundance.

Will you put your life into the hands of your Guide? Will you trust your Good Shepherd to lead you? Will you choose, despite the rocky terrain, to trust that I am leading you to a good place...to a land flowing with milk and honey? I see the end from the beginning; I see each path and where it leads. And I have chosen the path that is the absolute best for you because I love you dearly. Will you trust Me?

"My sheep listen to My voice; I know them, and they follow Me." John 10:27 (NIV)

Raise your sights, My child. You have allowed your gaze to drift from Me to all the hardships around you and the struggles that you face. The cares of this world have begun to choke the very life out of you.

But if you will cast your gaze heavenward and once again allow your eyes to rest and focus on Me, I will bring My order to the disheveled chaos of your life. I will take the cares that weigh so heavily upon you and uproot them as you entrust your life to Me once more. I will cause new growth to come from all the heavy rains under which you have been bearing up. I have protected you during the storms and been so very close beside you.

So, be strong, and take courage. Raise your sights to Me, My child. Set your face like flint as you turn your eyes in the direction of your loving Father and Deliverer.

You are My Church

"You are the light of the world. A city set on a hill cannot be hidden." Matt. 5:14

But there are those among you who would say they are of no import, are not effective or useful for service, or have nothing of value to bring...

To you, My child, I would say, I have called you and chosen you by name. I have grafted you into the body of Christ. Do not feel inadequate. Do not compare yourself with the gifts, talents, and exploits of others.

I have called you to come, to serve, and to bring the strengths with which I have uniquely blessed you; to do the works of righteousness that I have prepared before the beginning of time for you to walk in.

My child, you are My treasured possession... you are precious to Me. I have created you to serve as a unique joint in My body. And that which every joint supplies will enable My body to function according to My purpose and design.

My child, in your heart you have at times wandered to and fro, aimless and without direction. Your time of wandering has come to an end. For I am establishing you now; I am causing your roots to spread down deeply into rich soil so that you will be firmly planted.

And you will draw your nutrients and your drink from Me through the rich soil of My word, through the sun I shine upon you—which is My loving presence—and from the rain of the Holy Spirit with which I shower you.

They will make you strong and stable, able to withstand the winds that blow.

And in that place I will cause life and new growth to spring forth. The fruit that you bear will be good and sweet and abundant and will bring much glory to the Planter. And you will be known as the **planting of the Lord.**

"Count it all joy, my brothers, when you meet trials of various kinds, for you know that the testing of your faith produces [endurance]." Jas. 1:2-3

My child, if I choose to keep you in the storm, will you choose to trust Me to **keep** you in the storm? To **hold** you in the palm of My hand and carry you?

Receive My comfort now, knowing that I will care for you in the midst of the storm, knowing that I will never give you more than you can bear in My strength. I am not afar off—I am with you in the boat, holding you near.

Instead of looking at the waves, will you look for, and rejoice in, the evidences of My grace and intervention on your behalf all along this journey? You will see many if you will but recognize them.

Could I have chosen to take you a different, easier way? Yes. But am I working on your behalf in the midst of it, showing My care for you and helping you grow in your faith and trust in Me, growing you in perseverance and endurance?... absolutely!

Your children are precious to you, yet they are even more precious to Me...and I have a plan for their lives as well as for yours. You need to entrust them into My sure hands and loving care. Jeremiah 32:37-42 says:

"Behold I will gather them out of all the lands to which I have driven them in My anger, in My wrath, and in great indignation; and I will bring them back to this place and make them dwell in safety.

And they shall be My people, and I will be their God; and I will give them one heart and one way, that they fear Me always for their own good, and for the good of their children after them. And I will make an everlasting covenant with them that I will not turn away from them, to do them good; and I will put the fear of Me in their hearts so that they will not turn away from Me.

And I will rejoice over them to do them good, and I will faithfully plant them in this land with all My heart and with all My soul...so I am going to bring on them all the good that I am promising them." (NAS)

In faithfulness I called you; in faithfulness I will keep you; and in faithfulness I will sanctify you and present you as a spotless bride before My Father.

Take courage, little lamb, for I will carry you in My strong arms to the very end and **will not** let you go.

How could I ever forget the one I loved so much that I died for? For surely, your name **is** graven on My hands, and My nail scars are a constant reminder of My undying love for you and the price I paid to reconcile you to Myself.

How could I forget My precious child or walk away and abandon the one I gave My very life for? **Your** name, My precious child, is written **deeply** in My heart.

My children, do not shrink back from My presence. For who is it that condemns you? Even though your own heart condemns you, *I* am *greater* than your heart.

"But," you say, *"my sins are too great, too grievous for His sacrifice to atone for."* My beloved, do not be deceived, for I see the beginning from the end, and the end from the beginning. And I saw your present and future sins back at the cross.

Yet I chose you! Yet I died for you!

So come to Me; receive My love and forgiveness. For I love you with an *undying* and *unconditional* love, and I long for you to come as the bridegroom longs for his bride!

"Now all glory to God who is able to keep you from falling away and will bring you with great joy into His glorious presence without a single fault." Jude 1:24 (NLT)

My dear child, you feel like your faith may not survive this trial you're enduring—like you're losing your grip and hanging on by a thread—like your hand is slipping from Mine. Your very faith has been shaken to the core.

But I will not let you go. My grip is firm and sure, and My power is strong enough to hold you and keep you from falling even when yours has grown limp and weak.

Though the earth gives way and the mountains fall into the sea, My love for you is unshakable. When everything else in your life is crumbling, My love for you will be your footing to keep your steps sure.

Listen to the words of this song, and let them minister peace to your soul:

O wondrous love that will not let me go

I cling to You with all my strength and soul Yet if my hold should ever fail

This wondrous love will never let me go I'm resting in the everlasting arms

In the ever faithful heart The Shepherd of my life

You'll carry me on Your mighty wings of grace Keeping me until the day

I look into Your eyes

"The Lord your God is with you, the Mighty Warrior who saves. He will take great delight in you; in His love He will no longer rebuke you, but will rejoice over you with singing." Zeph. 3:17 (NIV)

I have a picture in my mind of a child snuggled in her father's lap, resting and receiving her daddy's love. But, she keeps jumping down because she sees other things in the room that allure and entice her and are calling for her attention.

I believe the Lord would say this morning:

Come, My little one. Your Father is waiting…waiting to comfort you, shower you with My love, and soothe you in My warm embrace.

Remain here, dear one, enfolded in My arms.

You are so quick to get down and rush on into the events of your day, but each and every task would benefit beyond measure by you remaining here just a few moments longer and gaining your strength from My love.

Remain a while longer and let Me sing over you of the greatness of My love for, and My delight in, you.

"If a man [has a] hundred sheep and one of them [goes astray], doth he not leave the ninety and nine, and goeth into the mountains, and seeketh that which is gone astray?" Matt. 18:12b (KJV)

You are that one, My child. You have been in the fold of My love. But now you have wandered far. In your heart you have gone far from the safety that I have for you, and this morning you find yourself high up in the rocky cliffs, trapped in a thorny thicket of the sin into which you have carelessly wandered.

You ask yourself, "How did I even get myself here?" You've gotten yourself so entangled that you don't even know where to begin in order to get yourself loose.

Maybe you've even managed to hide this from those around you who love you, but I know.

My child, it is **you** whom I leave the fold for this morning. It is **you** whom I seek.

I see where you are there, caught up in the briars. Will you let me free you this morning? Will you turn from your wanderings and will you return with Me this day?

I love you, My child, and I'll not give up until I bring you home!

Picture with Me this morning a battered, clay vessel, a vessel with many cracks and even holes. Through these cracks and holes, filthy, stagnant water is leaking out.

Maybe you feel like that cracked, holey vessel this morning. Maybe you even think of yourself as "damaged goods," a vessel many would say has no value or purpose whatsoever, a vessel to be disregarded, a vessel of shame and reproach.

But I would say to you, dear one, ***that*** *is the very vessel I wish to redeem.* ***You*** *are the very vessel I wish to redeem!*

As you submit yourself to Me and allow Me to empty you of that filthy stagnant water of self and allow Me to pour My Holy Spirit into you, it is those very holes and cracks, those broken parts of you, those weaknesses that you consider a shame and a reproach, that I will cause My **glory** to flow through and bring life to others.

For in your weakness, My power is perfected!

"The hand of the LORD was upon me, and He brought me out in the Spirit of the LORD and set me down in the middle of the valley; it was full of bones.
And He led me around among them and behold there were very many on the surface of the valley, and behold, they were very dry. And He said to me, 'Son of man, can these bones live?' And I answered, 'O Lord GOD, You know.'
Then He said to me, 'Prophesy over these bones, and say to them, O dry bones, hear the word of the LORD. Thus says the Lord GOD to these bones: Behold, I will cause breath to enter you and you shall live. And I will lay sinews upon you, and will cause flesh to come upon you, and cover you with skin, and put breath in you, and you shall live, and you shall know that I am the LORD.'" Ezek. 37:1-6

My child, perhaps this is an accurate description of the state of your heart this day—a barren valley filled with dry bones, and void of life.

My desire this morning is to penetrate your heart. I want to declare My love to you.

I want you to feel and experience My presence. I want to breathe new life into your spirit and cause your dry bones to rise up out of the dust and live.

I am the fountain of life, and I will water all your dry places. As the woman at the well came thirsty but left satisfied, so I call you to come now and drink freely. As often as you drink from My fountain of life, I will fill you—not give you just enough to get by—but saturate you with My goodness and faithfulness, and immerse you in the depths of My grace, pouring upon you of My Spirit. Only I can do this. You cannot will it to be so. But you must yield to Me and let Me do this work in you. Cry out to Me a desperate prayer from a sincere heart, and I will raise up your dry bones in newness of life, and you will dance before Me with joy!

"Seek the Lord while He may be found; call upon Him while He is near. Let the wicked forsake his way, and the unrighteous man his thoughts; let him return to the Lord, that He may have compassion on him, and to our God, for He will abundantly pardon." Isa. 55:6-7

Yes, My child I **will** abundantly pardon. For this is My heart toward you: grace, mercy and forgiveness.

What sin consumes your thoughts right now and looms before your guilty conscience?

I knew about that sin as I hung on the cross for you, and I covered it there with My blood.

Don't you know that, even before the world began, I saw your sin—in its entirety—but I had a plan to draw you to Myself, to save you from the penalty for those sins, and to call you My very own?

"I have swept away your offenses like a cloud, your sins like the morning mist. Return to Me, for I have redeemed you!" Isa. 44:22 (NIV)

There are those who desire to come but would say, "My sin is too great. I am not worthy."

But am I not the God of Reconciliation? That is Who I am! And was it not your sin that I died for? So come, My child, and bring your sin with you...but leave it at the foot of My cross.

"There is therefore now no condemnation for those who are in Christ Jesus." Rom. 8:1

"My grace is sufficient for you, for My power is made perfect in weakness." II Cor. 12:9

I believe the Lord would say, Yes, My child, My grace is sufficient for you…it is enough!

There is nothing stronger than My forgiveness of you…forgiveness you did not deserve and forgiveness that you could never earn.

That's My precious grace toward you, My child, and that grace is powerful enough to hold you close to Me, even when you fear you will fall away.

And that grace is strong enough to sustain you and bear you up even when you feel like giving up.

And My amazing grace will carry you like strong arms, even when you're afraid you'll stumble.

No sin you do can lessen My love for you- because I saved you by My grace, and I will keep you by My grace.

I have called you child, and you are Mine **forever**!!

My child, you hunger and thirst, yet you have no silver. Your cup is empty, yet you have no gold. You say, "I am empty and poured out"...but, My child, that is a good thing...for only an *empty* cup can I *fill*. It is only when your cup is empty that I can fill it with My sweet wine, with the joy and peace of My presence, with life itself!

So, empty yourself before Me--pour out your own life, your will, your fears, all the things of this world that you cling to so tightly and count so dear. *Then*, I will fill you with a new wine-- a wine *so* sweet—and with life like you've never known—for I will fill you with *Myself*, and you will never want for anything else.

Blessed are you if you hunger and thirst after Me...for you *will be filled!*

"But now thus says the Lord, He who created you, O Jacob, He who formed you, O Israel: Fear not, for I have redeemed you; I have called you by name, you are Mine." Isa. 43:1

In this new day, remember that **you are Mine**. I bought you at an outrageous price—the life of My one, dearly beloved, precious Son. Not that there was anything inherently worthy or lovely in you, but because it was My good pleasure to save you.

Through the corridors of time, I looked and saw you and I said, "**That** one I desire to be My child." And I called you by your name and opened your eyes to My fathomless love for you, demonstrated on the cross, and I drew you to Myself and adopted you as My very own.

Enter into this day, and every day, embracing the security of this truth…you are fully known and deeply, deeply loved by Me, both now and forever.

The Candle's Flame

Candles hold a beauty all their own. Not only do they give us light, but there is a quality about a candle's light, which many people find romantic and mysterious. They are used not only to give light but also to bring pleasure and to create a special ambiance or quality of atmosphere for aesthetic pleasure, and some are even used for their aromatic fragrance to fill a room with their perfume.

Each person God has created can be likened to one of these candles.

All have a wick within them, which is their heart of hearts. Many walk around all of their lives without the wick within them ever being ignited into flame because only the Lamp Lighter can light the wick…yet they refuse Him. Only Jesus can bring the heart, or spirit, to life. Those who refuse Him cannot give off any light of their own unless touched by His hand.

Those candles that choose to remain unlit never fulfill the purpose for which they were created…to bring forth light…to give glory to God.

Then there are those who have been brought to flame by His almighty hand, yet now the fire that once burned brightly when freshly lit is but a flicker, and it wanes and smokes as if almost extinguished. This candle must yield itself to the Lamp Lighter to have the wax (flesh) cut away from the wick (heart). The wax must be pared away to reveal more of the wick, which must be necessarily exposed in order to keep the candle's fire burning.

"Oh Lord, light the wick within my heart, that I may fulfill the purpose for which you created me—to give You glory and to shine Your splendid light amid the darkness of this world. Lord, please cut away what you must of my flesh and expose my heart, that my fire and passion for You may never wane. May my flame grow ever brighter as it is fanned by the wind of Your Spirit…that what began as the fire of one small candle would not only be used by You to light the wicks of others but would spread into a magnificent, raging fire across our land, and the world, for Your glory."

There are some this morning who could best be described as frightened little children. Not only have the cares of this world rolled in like a dark cloud and choked out your peace and joy, but your heart is troubled and fearful about circumstances you face.

Just as you earthly parents relate to your own precious children, My desire this morning is not to scold you but to comfort you. My desire is to draw you up on My knee and to let you feel My strong arms wrapped around you and to reassure you that you are safe within those powerful, loving arms. My desire is to remind you this morning of My total and complete sovereignty—My absolute control over everything that happens in your life—and My promise to work **all** of these things for your good.

Do not fear, little children, for your Father holds you tightly in His hands.

"Peace I leave with you; My peace I give to you; not as the world gives, do I give to you. Let not your hearts be troubled, neither let them be afraid." John 14:27

"As for man, his days are like grass. He flourishes like a flower of the field; for the wind passes over it, and it is gone, and its place knows it no more." Ps. 103:15-16

My child, a moment just passed and can never be retrieved. And yet another just passed and cannot be relived. And another is as vapor, vanished, gone forever.

I implore you, My child, to live **each** moment of **every** day for Me, seeing My purpose for your life, My purpose for you in that moment.

The things you have been striving for, pouring yourself into, and setting your hopes upon—your education, your career, your personal ambitions— these will all die with you.

You have but one chance to live this next moment, hour, day, week— live it for My glory, following My will, My purpose for your life, the path that **I** have set before you, **My will** in the moment. Then you will have no regrets, for only the things done for Christ will last.

Holy Spirit, I ask that You would penetrate the crusty exterior of my hardened heart. Lord, You have given me a new heart, and I ask that, right now, You would break up any of the crust that I have allowed to form around it.

Lord, I ask that my heart would be open to receive Your Word…words of encouragement and words of love.

Lord, I would also pray that Your holiness would sweep through me. I pray that the brightness and light of Your glory would illuminate me, would amaze me, and would set me ablaze once again in order that I would, once again, reflect Your glory, the hope of heaven, the peace that comes from rest in You, and the joy that comes only from abiding in Your presence, to a lost and dying world.

ome, all you who hunger and thirst. You've had, perhaps, much food and drink in the last few days, but they have not fulfilled the longing of your heart. The longing of your heart is a place that I have reserved for Myself to fill. And I say unto you that nothing else will ever fill that longing, because I have reserved it for Myself…to fill that place with My very presence and My love.

And it has been an evidence of My mercy toward you that you continue to feel this hunger and thirst. I have chosen not to allow you to be filled and satisfied by the things of this world so that you would continue to crave and seek after Me. The things that you have tasted have not filled you, because your very desire was given to you by Me.

And it's that craving that I long to fulfill. And it's that hunger, that thirst, that I **will** fulfill. It's a yearning that will continue and a deep desire that will continually be satisfied…not just once, but time and time again.. And as much as you are filled, I will fill you again and again…because that is Who I am. I am your infinite Father. I am your loving Father. My love is endless, and My well knows no end and no limits, and I am creating within you a greater capacity to experience My love.

"On the last and greatest day of the feast, Jesus stood and said in a loud voice, 'If anyone is thirsty, let him come to Me and drink.
Whoever believes in Me, as the Scripture has said, streams of living waters will flow from within him.' By this He meant the Spirit, whom those who believed in Him were later to receive."
John 7:37-39a (NAS)

Lord, we thank you for all that we have received from Your gracious hand. Help us, Lord…we need Your help to be grateful and to be joyful…to be contented regardless of the situations and circumstances we find ourselves in, circumstances that are guaranteed to change. Lord, we want our confidence, our contentment, and our joy to be founded in You and You alone.

Lord, what a hope that You've called us to. More than we could ask or imagine are the blessings that You seek to lavish upon us. Lord, let our hearts be receptive and open to all that You want to do in us and through us. Lord, we pray that You would create in us, as only You can, hungry hearts. Lord, create in us hearts that are utterly desperate for You, that we might have the passion that Paul had just to give You glory, that we, too, would start our days pondering all that You have done for us and of Your great promises which You have made to us. Lord, we ask that our passion would be to bring glory to You and to Your great Name, and that we would not be content until we're growing in You.

Lord, give us an increased passion for You, for Your sweet presence, and for the glory of Your Name, that we might be given to Your mission on this earth. We sense Your Spirit moving as we hear reports of what You are doing in the world today…it makes our hearts aware of our thirst for even greater things, O God. We want to pray big prayers for all that You desire to do and for how You will use us in Your great plan. Lord, we want to be in the middle of the river as Your Spirit flows, not cautiously on one side or the other but fully in the middle; not just dipping our toes in but completely immersed in what Your Holy Spirit is doing.

But Lord, we cry out in desperation. This is nothing we can do in ourselves, nothing we can manufacture on our own. O Lord, we ask Your Holy Spirit to come and minister, that You would lead us day by day as You led the children of Israel with the cloud and the pillar of fire, that we would follow You, that we would stop when it's time to stop, that we would go when it's time to go, and that we would follow You all of our days. Lord, let that be our passion and our cry. Lord, right now we just stop and we declare our love for You.

My children, I would say to you that until now you have really asked Me for very little. But I would urge you to ask of Me. Ask anything according to My will, and I will give it to you. And My will is for you to ask for more of Me.

I would say to you this morning that in the days ahead I will be pouring out My Spirit upon you; I will be giving you more of Me than you've ever experienced before. So I tell you today, ask to be thirsty…ask for an increase in your thirst for Me…ask for an increase in your passion for Me.

Some of you have even wondered, "Can I even be passionate for God? Can I really even love Him as I should?" Ask of Me, and I will give you the passion that you have been lacking. Ask of Me, and I will fill you with My own love…the great love that I have for My Son, Jesus, which I now lavish upon you because of His substitutionary death for you. You will begin to taste My passion for Him.

So ask to be thirsty; ask to be hungry. I promise you that I will come and I will fill you; I will fill you afresh. And you, too, will know the joy of My presence. You will know the joy of seeking Me with all your heart and finding Me. This is My promise to you…ask, begin to ask, and I will fill the longings of your heart, because I am the One who will place those longings deep within you in response to your prayers.

"See what great love the Father has lavished on us, that we should be called children of God!" I John 3:1a (NIV)

My child, are you yearning for a love that is an illusion? Are you seeking a human love, with all of its imperfections, to satisfy a spiritual longing?

"Love" like this will leave you wanting and even more desperate when you find that what you had hoped would fulfill you has left you even emptier than ever.

Maybe you have now My love, but its effect on your heart has waned. Receive My love afresh this morning. Let it cover you as a warm blanket and flow over your heart as soothing, comforting oils.

You are known completely… And loved perfectly!

"I, even I, am the One who wipes out your transgressions for My own sake; and I will not remember your sins." Isa. 43:25

Whiter than freshly fallen snow…that is how I see you now, My child. For I have blotted out your sins, **all** of them, so completely that there is **no** trace of them left. And I have declared that I will no longer consider them or hold them against you **ever**!

You now stand clean before Me. I see **no blemish** on you, not stain **at all**.

So come freely, with confidence, without any fear of rejection or condemnation. For who is there that can condemn you when the almighty, holy God has completely forgiven you?

You say, "My God, how far away you are from me today," as if My presence were something I desire to withhold from you for some reason. But am I not just as close as I have ever been? I long to be with you, My child!

I will never leave you nor forsake you; though at times you may not be aware of My presence with you, I am always by your side.

Rest…cease from striving and rest…You run anxiously, you try to do more to please Me, you try to pray just the right words.

How it grieves My heart as your Father that you are afraid of Me turning My back on you, you fear me becoming angry with you and withdrawing My presence.

Don't frantically strive for My presence as if it is something you can work up somehow by mental assent, or something you can earn if you are good enough to deserve it, or do enough to please Me. Apart from Christ, you will never be deserving of My presence, but it is something I desire to give to you. I, your Father, want to be with you even more than you desire to be with Me.

Please stop striving and simply rest…rest in the knowledge of My great love for you as your Father. Come and just enjoy what I am seeking to lavish upon you. I gently lead you by the still and quiet waters and bid you to come and rest with Me.

Oh, My child, if you only knew how often you are on My mind. Night and day you are before Me. You could not even begin to count My many precious thoughts of you, so vast is the sum of them. There is never a moment that My gaze doesn't rest upon you, My beloved.

Oh, the joy that floods My heart when you return that gaze, and our eyes meet as we share sweet communion together and drink deeply the cup of fellowship. It delights My heart at these times to pour out upon you My rich, satisfying presence and the thirst quenching refreshment of My Spirit. Come and dine, come and feast at My table of sweet communion and you will be satisfied. Your peace and joy will be renewed, your hope restored, and you will not be in want for any good thing.

Remember, child, My eyes are forever upon you…

"Who is a God like Thee, who pardons iniquity and passes over the rebellious act of the remnant of His possession? He does not retain His anger forever, because He delights in unchanging love. He will again have compassion on us; He will tread our sins underfoot. Yes, Thou wilt cast all their iniquities into the depths of the sea. Thou will give truth to Jacob, and unchanging love to Abraham." Mic. 7:18-20

My child, your heart is not so hard that the power of my love and forgiveness cannot shatter it; nor is the fortress that you've built around your heart able to withstand my penetrating, unchanging love toward you. I will dissolve it away with My tears of compassion for you, and I will woe you with My still small, tender voice.

Who is a God like Me, who delights in forgiving all your sins and rebellion, and in having compassion on you according to His unchanging love?

Allow this truth to shatter your walls; allow My unchanging love toward you to crush them and make your heart soft and tender toward Me.

And she will sing there as in the days of her youth, as in the day when she came up from the land of Egypt. Hos. 2:16

My child, I am here with you this morning. I have never left your side, nor will I ever go away from you. Open your heart to me now and rejoice in the sweetness of My presence as you have in times past. Come once again to the cool, refreshing waters. Drink from my clear, never-ending fountain and feel the life of My Spirit flowing through you once again, washing away the dry dusty valleys within and restoring the lakes and rivers of fresh water from which you, and others, may draw and be blessed.

Once again as you draw from My water of life, you will see new growth and beauty springing forth in the wilderness of your heart. You will see all the barren places covered once again with luscious foliage and rich new life.

My presence is here with you, surrounding you even now.

Open your heart wide and drink deeply of My life-giving water.

My child, are you more aware as you stand before Me this morning of your sins, or of the forgiveness of your sins? Are you more aware of your failures and mistakes, or of the blood of My Son which covers them **all** and washes you clean of them?

Remember, My sons and daughters, remember who I am...for I am your **Father**, not a harsh or temperamental god which you must appease. I have not dealt with you as you deserve. Instead of My wrath, I've poured out My love for you. Instead of harshness, I've shown you tenderness, compassion and kindness. Instead of judgment, I've shown you mercy and grace.

My children, I am the almighty God, but to you I am also your tenderhearted Father and you stand before me this morning completely forgiven.

Remember this...

Still your anxious thoughts, My child…calm your heart and rest in Me, trust in Me. You may feel as though the world is spinning out of control for yourself or for those you love…you may feel that things are falling apart…but did I not know about this before time began?

In this time of trouble, have I not made a way of escape? Though you feel weak and powerless to effect change, lean on My strength. In this time of hopelessness, fill your heart with the hope that I give. In this time of turbulence, lift your eyes to look at your Redeemer…I redeemed your life from the pit, cannot I even redeem this situation? Is it so dire that My hand cannot save?

See all things with the eyes of faith. Humble yourself before Me, submit this situation and all of those involved to Me, come under the authority of My mighty hand…and trust Me.

"He will not let your foot be moved; He who keeps you will not slumber nor sleep….The Lord is your keeper." Ps. 121:3-5a

"Sing to the Lord a new song, for He has done marvelous things; His right hand and His holy arm have worked salvation for Him. The Lord has made His salvation known and revealed His righteousness to the nations.
He has remembered His love and His faithfulness to the house of Israel." Ps. 98:1-3

Yes, I have done marvelous things for you, My child. I have poured out My blessing upon you lavishly. But there have been days when you have said in your heart, "God cannot bless me today because of my unfaithfulness and inconsistency toward Him." Then there have been other days when you have thought, "Today His blessings will flow toward me because I have spent much time in prayer and reading His word. Because I have been faithful, He will be faithful toward me."

My child, My blessings flow from the very heart of grace from which your salvation came. You do not, and never will, deserve My favor and My blessings. You deserved only death, but I gave you life, and that abundantly, through the death of My Son for you. You deserved only wrath, but I have poured out My blessings upon you...even in times when you have been unfaithful. And have I not said that all your righteousness is as filthy rags in My sight? My blessings are not dependent upon your performance, your faithfulness, your righteousness...but upon My righteousness which now covers you in Christ.

So, receive My blessings which I have, and will continue, to lavish upon you with a grateful heart...but know that they flow, not because of anything you have or have not done, but rather from My heart of undeserved grace toward you.

As you therefore have received Christ Jesus the Lord, so walk in Him, having been firmly rooted and now being built up in Him and established in your faith. Col. 2:6-7

I have led you to this place for a purpose, My child...It is by design and My grace that you are here...For it is My desire to train you in *godliness* and to *refine* your *character* for My glory and for the furtherance of My Kingdom... to set your roots *firmly* and *deeply* into the riches of the soil of My word from which you will draw *stability* and *strength* so that when the winds blow *you will not be shaken*, but will be able to *stand firm in your faith*. I have brought you to this place to raise you up into a *mighty oak* to which the world can run for shelter and shade and to find rest for their souls within your branches. I am molding you into a refuge, a harbor, a resting place...if you will yield to My gentle hand and allow Me to fashion you according to *My* will...

For My desire is to refine you into a beautiful diamond, and though the process may be painful as I chip away at the flaws in your character that you can't even see, the end result will be a stunning jewel which will show the world My glory. Let Me fashion, let Me chisel, let Me show the world My glory through a magnificent precious stone which I have called My own and love enough to work with so carefully and with such skill, patience and tenacity. You will *shine* for My glory!

"Christin you, the hope of glory." Col. 1:27

My child, I love you so much. Love is a word so overused, but My love for you far exceeds any you have ever known, for it is unconditional and eternal, it is limitless and ever flowing toward you. Love for you compelled Me to the cross to secure your redemption. It is also because of My great love for you that I have gone before you to prepare a place for you, that you will one day soon be with Me always. I am anxiously waiting for you on the other side, my heart yearning to be with you face to face, anticipating our joyous reunion, and looking forward to showing you around this spectacular place which I've prepared for you, and to sharing in your delight and wonder and awe.

Does your heart yearn for Me as Mine does for you, My love? Does anticipation of seeing Me face to face make your heart beat faster as it does Mine? Does the hope of heaven swell your heart with renewed courage and strength to carry on? Look heavenward to the One who loves and waits for you.

S ome this morning would say,

"Yes, it is finished…but is it enough? Is it enough to cover me, to cover my sins? Is it enough to cover my failures? Is it enough to cover my weaknesses?"

My child, when I said, 'It is finished', I meant it is totally completed, it is completely enough…completely finished and more than enough for all who would turn their hearts humbly toward Me…completely finished and more than enough to cover you.

Remember My words in Psalm 103, because they are for you, My child. Grab hold of them and cling to their truths!

"Bless the Lord, and forget none of His benefits Who pardons all your sins Who heals all your diseases Who redeems your life from the pit Who crowns you with lovingkindness and compassion Who satisfies your years with good things, so that your youth is renewed like the eagle."

O My child, it is not only <u>finished</u>, it is more than enough for <u>you!</u>

"Take heed to the ministry which you have received in the Lord, that you may fulfill it." Col. 4:17

My children, I have given to each of you various gifts...gifts to be used in ministry to Me; gifts to be used in ministering to My people; gifts to be used to reach a lost world with the hope of salvation.

There is one body, yet many parts, each with a unique function; and that which every joint supplies is vital to the working or the whole.

I would ask this morning, is there any lack in the body that exists because you are not fulfilling the ministry to which I have called you? Is there a weakness in any area because you are not using your God-given ministry, gifting or talent? Are you holding back waiting to see if another will step in and accomplish the task – But I have called you!

Are you gifted in hospitality? Then ask how you may use it to further My kingdom. Are you gifted as an evangelist? Then look for the opportunities I send your way and seize each one. Do you have the gift of prophecy? Then regularly ask Me what I desire to speak to My people.

This is not a stern word, but rather a gentle reminder, that the gifts which you have been given were given to you by Me and for My glory, and to further My kingdom. Be faithful with what you have been given and I will bless you with even more.

I chose you, My child, before you breathed your first breath of life. Even before I formed the heavens and the earth I knew your name and I chose you and called you to be Mine. And not only did I know your name, but I saw all of your days from your first to your last. I saw ahead to every sin you would commit, every act of rebellion against Me, every area of temptation you would struggle with, and yet, even being fully aware of all these things, I still chose you from the foundations of the world to be My precious child.

I chose you, I called you, I made a way through the death of My son, Jesus, to cleanse you of all your sin in order to reconcile you to Myself, and I will keep you in the palm of My great hand until the day I return to take you home with Me.

Yes, Mine is a wondrous, wondrous love that will not let you go. If only you knew the depths of it you would never again doubt it!

Look forward, My child, to that day of My return, for I'm coming back for you, and may joy fill your heart at the thought of this!

"For the Lord Himself will descend from heaven with a shout, with the voice of the archangel, and with the trumpet of God, and the dead in Christ shall rise first. Then we who are live and remain shall be caught up together with them in the clouds to meet the Lord in the air, and thus we shall always be with the Lord. Therefore comfort one another with these words." I Thess. 4:16-18

"Trust in the Lord with all your heart and lean not on your own understanding; in all your ways acknowledge Him, and He will direct your paths." Prov. 3:5-6

My child, do you not know that I have called you. And if I have called you will I not help you also? I will not leave you alone to grope in the dark trying to find your own way. What Father would allow His child to be lost and helpless and not help him find his way. Know that when you ask for My help, and when you seek for My guidance and wisdom, and when you search for My will...I will certainly reveal to you the way to go. For I desire nothing more than for you to walk in My ways and to walk according to My will for your life—for that is the path which brings Me the greatest glory. Know, My child, that I will lead you. Trust in Me.

"He who dwells in the shelter of the Most High will abide in the shadow of the Almighty. I will say to the Lord, 'My refuge and my fortress, My God, in whom I trust!' For it is He who delivers you from the snare of the trapper, and from the deadly pestilence. He will cover you with His pinions, and under His wings you may seek refuge; His faithfulness is a shield and bulwark.

You will not be afraid of the terror by night, or of the arrow that flies by day; of the pestilence that stalks in darkness, or of the destruction that lays waste at noon. A thousand may fall at your side, and ten thousand at your right hand; but it shall not approach you. You will only look on with your eyes, and see the recompense of the wicked. For you have made the Lord, my refuge, even the Most High, your dwelling place.

No evil will befall you, nor will any plague come near your tent. For He will give His angels charge concerning you, to guard you in all your ways.

They will bear you up in their hands, lest you strike your foot against a stone. You will tread upon the lion and cobra, the young lion and the serpent you will trample down.

'Because He has loved Me, therefore I will deliver him; I will set him securely on high, because he has known My name. He will call upon Me, and I will answer him; I will be with him in trouble; I will rescue him, and honor him. With a long life I will satisfy him, and let him behold My salvation.' Ps. 91:1-16

My little child, what fear grips your heart this morning? Of what are you afraid? Are these things greater than I, I who created you, I who formed the mountains and the mighty seas with a breath, who spoke the world into existence and all it contains, who holds the universe in My hands...is that which you fear <u>greater</u> than I?

I would say to you this morning, do not fear, do not be afraid, as those who do not know me and who have no hope. Place your hope and trust in Me this morning; do not look to another for your help...don't look to your riches...for not only am I the Almighty God, but I am your loving Father, and I am mighty to save! Will I not surely help you now, My little child?

My child, your life is like a breath, a vapor that lasts only a moment then is gone. Your time on this earth is short. Are you waking each morning with a goal to reflect My glory to a dying world? Are you walking through each day with a heavenward gaze and asking "Lord, how can I advance and further Your Kingdom this day? How would you use me today to accomplish your eternal purposes?" Only the things for Christ will last when the vapor of your life is gone. Seek each day to leave a legacy that will bring glory to My Name and accomplish My glorious will.

I have ***rescued*** you, My child. I have rescued you.

Once you were alone, and I have brought you into My house. You were abandoned, but I brought you into My family.

You were an orphan, but I made you a son, and an heir...I gave you a glorious heritage. You were dressed in threadbare, hole-filled clothes; but I have dressed you with My glorious garments of righteousness. Let your heart be filled with gratefulness and gratitude this morning for all the wonderful things I've done in your life!

"But our citizenship is in heaven, and from it we await a Savior, the Lord Jesus Christ." Phil. 3:20

The Kingdom of Heaven is at hand. Eternity is very close to you. Don't think of heaven as some faraway place, so far removed from the world that you live in...for just beyond the temporal world that you see is the eternal glories of My Heaven that you cannot see.

Heaven lies just beyond the veil of the temporal, just beyond what your eyes now behold...heaven is just a breath away. Live your life with an awareness that heaven is very close at hand.

"Nevertheless, the firm foundation of God stands, having this seal, 'The Lord knows those who are His.'" 2 Tim. 2:19a

My child, not only do I know you more truly and intimately than any other ever has or ever will, I also love you more deeply than any other ever could.

The promises I made to you through My Word upon your salvation— the true and precious promises that I set as a firm foundation before the world began—those promises are just as sure today for you as they were when I first spoke them to your heart. I will never leave you nor forsake you.

Lo, I will be with you always, even unto the ends of the earth. I will guide you and direct your paths!

I am calling you this morning to stand secure upon the firm foundation of My promises. Trust in My Word. Trust in My love. Trust in My faithfulness.

"For you will go out with joy, and be led forth with peace; the mountains and the hills will break forth into shouts of joy before you, and all the trees of the field will clap their hands. Instead of the thorn bush, the cypress will spring forth and grow; and instead of the nettle, the myrtle will come up." Isa. 55:12-13

My child, is this **your** outlook or your perspective on your life in Christ? Is this the spiritual glasses which you view your life through?

Do you **believe** that My plans are for your good, not for evil; to bless you and not to harm you? Do you have your hope firmly planted in Me and in My goodness, faithfulness, and My love? Do you hold firmly in your heart that I have a glorious future prepared for you?

Or do you expect thorn bushes to spring up and evil to befall you, maybe because you still see yourself covered with the stain of your sin instead of covered by My righteousness and wrapped in My grace?

O may you say with the Psalmist this morning: Why so downcast O my soul?

Put your hope in God!

In my mind, I see a picture of a boat out on the sea, caught up in the middle of a great storm...waves crashing down upon it, tossing it to and fro. It reminds me of the story in the Bible in which the disciples and Jesus were crossing the sea and entered into such a storm. Jesus slept peacefully while the white-knuckled disciples were terrified for their very lives. When they woke Jesus, he simply stretched out His hand and said, Peace, be still, and the storm grew calm immediately.

There are some this morning who identify quite readily with those white-knuckled disciples. The trials, troubles, and terrors of life seem to be crashing down upon you, tossing you about relentlessly. And while we are reminded by this story that our sovereign Lord is all powerful, is in control of everything that happens to us in our lives, and has authority to calm the storm that is pounding us, sometimes He chooses instead to draw us near, and to hold us tightly to Himself, and to carry us through the storm to the other side. As the song puts it so well...

'Sometimes He calms the storm, and other times He calms His child.'

"Peace I leave with you; My peace I give you. I do not give to you as the world gives. Do not let your hearts be troubled and do not be afraid." John 14:27

"You will keep him in perfect peace whose mind is steadfast because he trusts in You." Isa. 26:3 (AKJV)

What anxious thoughts and worries cloud your mind this morning, My little one? What cares and concerns weigh heavy on your heart?

Now is the time for you to come to Me...I am waiting here in the Holy Place for *you*. Now is the time for you to enter into the presence of your Father and to allow Me to loose the burdens that stoop you over...to once again set your heart free and your spirit to flight, and to once again allow My joy and peace to engulf you.

And I will *keep* you in this place of peace, even as new trials come, if you will continue to meet Me here in the secret place, if you will *abide* in Me, if you will turn your thoughts to Me in prayer and cast all your cares at My feet.

And you will find that though the storm rages, you are safe beneath the shelter of My wings and unmovable upon a high rock that *cannot* be shaken.

Yes, My child, I *will* keep you in perfect peace if your mind is stayed on Me.

"Now may the God of peace Himself sanctify you entirely; and may your spirit and soul and body be preserved complete, without blame at the coming of our Lord Jesus Christ. Faithful is He who calls you, and He also will bring it to pass!!" I Thess. 5:23-24

My child, why do you feel that you have gone too far away from Me to hear My voice calling to you   too   far away in your heart to return to Me?

Know this—that My voice is calling to you this day— will you hear it? Sometimes I whisper deep in your heart, "Come unto Me, My child." But other times I cry out in a loud voice through trials and difficulties in your life, imploring for you to return to Me.

No, My child, you are not gone so far that you cannot come back, for I see I see your heart and the places it has wandered to. And wherever you do run, know that I will pursue you there because I love you. I will never let you go. My arms are continually outstretched toward you, longing to embrace you.

So, My child, do not harden your heart to My voice this day but come, return to Me, that you might receive new life, fresh peace, and joy that knows no bounds!

On the night Jesus was betrayed, He took His disciples to the garden of Gethsemane with Him and asked them to keep watch and pray. One, two, three times he returned to find them fast asleep.

I believe the Lord would say to some this morning, just as He did to His disciples in the garden that night:

Keep watch and pray, so that you will not fall into temptation. For I have found you sleeping yet again. There is a subtle indifference that has crept in, and sleep has gradually come upon and overtaken you. Your faith has weakened, and there has developed a gradual distance between you and I, not in My heart, but in yours.

Yet, I am still waiting, arms open like a father to receive His dear child…waiting for you to shake off your slumber and turn and glance My way again; waiting for you to come running again to the One who loves you more than any other; waiting for you to see Me, not half-heartedly, but with your whole heart.

"Awake, O sleeper, and arise from the dead, and Christ will shine on you." Eph. 5:15

"Why so downcast, O my soul? Put your hope in God" Ps.
42:11

My Child, why is your soul downcast? You are looking to all your circumstances, all your decisions, all your difficulties... But I tell you to look to the long tomorrow.

Yes, cast your eyes heavenward and look to the skies, for one day soon I will return to take you home to be with Me forever...and today might be that very day. If it were today, would I find you sulking and downhearted with your head in your hands, or would I find your hands raised up in worship and praise to Me for all of My goodness, faithfulness and loving-kindness to you. For truly, haven't I been so good to you? Think on these things!

"Change me, O God," you cry. But you run into My presence, list your requests of Me, then leave. You do not linger, you do not wait, you do not rest and abide. You will be changed as you tarry in My presence and allow Me to do My work in your heart. You will be changed from glory to glory, that is, as you enter into My glorious presence and remain long enough for Me to touch your heart.

Your heart will be set aright when your eyes are set on Me.

The Lord gave me a picture this morning of a sailboat out in the middle of the ocean. There was not a wind at all, nor even a breeze, but the sea was as smooth as glass with not even a ripple, and the sails on the boat hung limp. The boat was stagnant, stuck in the water, and could not move at all.

I saw a man on the deck cupping his hands around his mouth and blowing frantically into the sails, trying to fill them with air to continue on his journey and make some progress in his travel...but to no avail.

Then I saw the heavens open and a mighty wind come down from heaven. It puffed out every sail fully and began to move the boat seemingly effortlessly in the direction it desired.

That boat represents some of our lives. We feel stagnant, dry, and seem to be making little or no progress on this journey of faith. We make every effort to do anything we can think of to fill our own sails, because we hate being in this place, but to no avail. Day after day, week after week, it seems we find ourselves unchanged, unmoved.

But the Lord is saying that it is a work that must be done by His Spirit. This morning the wind is changing, for the Lord is doing a new work in your heart by His Spirit. Let the wind of the Spirit fill your sails once again with new joy, new peace, refreshing, a knowledge of His love, renewed hope, vision and faith for the future. He is taking you onward this morning...He is moving you in the direction He desires for you. Trust in *Him* to do the work that you cannot do in your own heart, for He is faithful and He surely will do it.

O Lord, create in me a clean heart, and renew a right spirit within me. Let me be overwhelmed once again by the warmth of Your sweet presence and the delight of Your love.

Stoke the fires of my heart that have in any way grown dim, that they may burst into flame afresh and show forth Your glory from this earthen vessel into a darkened world that is so in need of Your light.

O My child, tender are My thoughts toward you. As a Father looks down lovingly and adoringly upon his little baby, so is My heart as I look upon you.

Receive My tender affection. Rest in My loving gaze, and find your heart warmed, your joy returned, and your strength renewed.

"...and lo, I am with you always, even to the end of the age."
Matt. 28:20b

Return to Me, My beloved Return to Me, My bride My child, I love you just as dearly As the day for you I died

And though your heart has drifted And your love for Me has waned My heart toward you, child Always will remain unchanged

And though this world with all its musings Has swept you so far out to sea Look up and see your Savior's face

For child, I am not far from **thee!**

"'For I know the plans that I have for you,' declares the Lord, 'plans for welfare and not for calamity, to give you a future and a hope.'" Jer. 29:11

This morning, are you weak and weary because you have lost your focus, you have lost your hope?

My child, My word is the same yesterday, today, and forever…and this verse still holds true for your life.

But you've become entangled and distracted by the day-to-day and the mundane, and have forgotten that you are called to a higher purpose, a heavenly purpose.

So I would remind you of that calling this morning. I would remind you of the good and wonderful plans that I have for you. I would remind you that your future is bright before you and your hope is sure.

Turn your eyes once again from the mundane tasks of everyday to the purpose for which you were created. For those who hope in the Lord will renew their strength!

O My children, I am speaking a fresh word to you…Yes, I am doing a new thing among you. I am creating within My people a passion for holiness. My holiness will be as a threshing floor, and I will use it to separate the wheat from the chaff.

I am calling you as wheat to come out from among the chaff and to be thoroughly separate unto Me. I have called you out of darkness into the light of My holiness.

Come unto Me, My people, and be purged in the fire of My all-consuming presence until all that remains is holy. Allow Me to change you from glory to glory into My image.

O My precious ones, in whom is all My delight...O that you would know the height, the width, the length, and the depth of My love. How great is My love for you! It is deeper than the deepest ocean. My love for you is higher than the highest mountain. It is wider than the widest sea.

What is there in all the earth that can possibly contain all the fullness of My love? And what is there that exists that can hide you from it? It is unsearchable, unfathomable, and limitless. My love for you is never ending and unchanging.

Never doubt My love for you, but rather hope in it...trust in it...rest in it.

My child, beautiful robes of righteousness, whiter than snow...this is what I have clothed you with. Why, then, do you see yourself as dressed in soiled, common clothes?

I have dressed you in royal clothing, as sons and daughters of the Most High God!

Why, then, do you insist on wearing the rags of a pauper?

Surely I say to you, do not call unclean that which I have made clean, and do not call unholy that which I have made holy. For you are the sons of the Most High God, and I see no stain upon you. I see you cleansed with the blood of My Son, whiter than snow, and I beckon you to come boldly into the presence of a holy God!

Hope of Glory

"My Father's house has many rooms; if that were not so, would I have told you that I am going there to prepare a place for you? And if I go and prepare a place for you, I will come back and take you to be with Me that you also may be where I am." John 1:2-3 (NIV)

My child, I would both challenge and encourage you this morning. Where are you placing your hope? What are you hoping in?

Have you forgotten that I promised to return for you? Have you forgotten the hope of heaven?

Have you forgotten that you are merely a stranger in this land passing through to a home infinitely more glorious?

Let this hope fill your heart anew and transform your thoughts from being consumed with this temporary world to dwelling upon your forever home with Me.

"But Zion said, 'The Lord has forsaken me; my Lord has forgotten me.' Can a woman forget her nursing child, that she should have no compassion on the son of her womb? Even these may forget, yet I will not forget you. Behold, I have engraved you on the palms of my hands." Isa. 49:14-16a

Beloved, I have never left your side.

Even in the quiet times, when you can't hear My voice, I am near. Even when the world and all its troubles are overwhelming your soul and its lies ringing loudly in your ears that I have forgotten you and abandoned you, I am still holding tightly to your hand and will never let go.

Remember My words to you and cling fast to them:

I will never leave you or forsake you. <u>Never</u>! <u>This</u> is truth. This is My promise and a rock on which you can stand.

I love you, and I am with you <u>always</u>!

A simple prayer

"*Good morning, My sweet Lord. What a joy to see You first thing in the morning and to feel the warm light of Your presence. Thank You for meeting me here. Thank you for washing me clean of all my sin and making me new so that I am worthy through the blood of Christ which covers me to come to You without reservation or hesitation into Your delightful presence as my loving Father.*"

O My child, come here often. Come often and drink of the refreshing water that I give you, for this is where your "life" comes from. There is an abundant river, a river of plenty that never runs dry, and which flows constantly from My throne. Come and drink of the sweet waters and be refreshed in your spirit and in your soul.

Enter to Possess...

"And You told them to go in to possess the land that You had sworn to give them." Neh. 9:15b

What is holding you back from entering the land I promised to give you? What report will you believe: that the giants of the land are too great? That the obstacles are too many? That you are not strong enough, talented enough, or don't have what it takes to be successful in what I am calling you to?

Or will you believe this report: I will go before you and make the rough places smooth. I will go behind you and be your rear guard. I will walk beside you, upholding you with the arm of My strength, and keep you from stumbling. I will bring the mountains low and raise up the valleys so that you have a straight and level path to walk out My good and perfect will for you. I will overcome the obstacles that you cannot. Rise up in the power and might of your God.

Enter and possess that which I have promised to give!

I am sensing that there are some this morning who are struggling with fear…particularly fear of falling away from the Savior you love, fear of drifting.

I believe God put this passage on my heart for you, to remind you that it was He who called you, and that it is He who will keep you, holding you fast and secure in His everlasting grip of grace.

I will lift up my eyes to the mountains; where does my help come from? My help comes from the Lord who made heaven and earth.
He will not allow your foot to slip. He who keeps you will not slumber…
….The Lord is your keeper. The Lord is your shade on your right hand. The sun will not smite you by day, nor the moon by night. The Lord will protect you from all evil; He will keep your soul.
The Lord will guard your going out and your coming in, from this time forth and forever. Ps. 121: 1-8 (NIV)

M

y *dear* child,

Precious...so precious...are you in My sight. All My thoughts toward you are loving-kindness, mercy, and grace. All My promises to you are **Yes** and **Amen**...Stand firm on them! Every word that I've spoken to your heart in the past, and every word that I've impressed on others to speak over you, these I will perform. For I am true to My word and true to My promises. What I have said, I will do. What I have proclaimed, I will perform. The good work I have begun in you to prepare you for these things I will finish and complete so that My word will be fulfilled and My glory will abound.

Trust in Me, rest and abide in My presence, and here let Me do the work of change in your heart. Draw in deeper, draw in closer... uninhibited, unrestrained, and without reservation...allow the fire of My presence to purify you as the most brilliant of gold and to skim away all impurities so that what remains will be a life to fulfill My purposes and a light that will shine for **Me**.

"So the ransomed of the Lord will return, and come with joyful shouting to Zion; and everlasting joy will be on their heads. They will obtain gladness and joy, and sorrow and sighing will flee away.

I, even I, am He who comforts you.

Who are you that you are afraid of man who dies, and the son of man who is made like grass; that you have forgotten the Lord your Maker, who stretched out the heavens, and laid the foundations of the earth; that you fear continually all day long because of the fury of the oppressor, as he makes ready to destroy? But where is the fury of the oppressor? The exile will soon be set free, and will not die in the dungeon, nor will his bread be lacking. For I am the Lord your God...and I have covered you with the shadow of My hand...you are My people."

Isa. 51:11-16

Yes, beloved, the enemy seeks your life...but do not fear! For I declare, says the Lord, that this trial will not destroy you. You feel as though you are being crushed, but I will not let this storm overtake you!

For this is going to make you stronger, if you cling to Me through it. Though the enemy fiercely assails you, he will not gain the victory over you! For I am the Lord your God, and I will be your defense, My precious child. I have hidden you beneath the shadow of My wings.

So do not lose your hope, and do not lose your vision—for I am with you in the storm!

And though sorrow may last for the night, a shout of joy will come with the morning light!

"And so we all, the veil having been removed from our faces, reflecting as a mirror the glory of God, are being changed and transformed into His image from glory to glory by the Spirit of the Lord." II Cor. 3:18

My *precious* child, do you look like your heavenly Father? Do you sound like Him, act like Him, have His ways about you? How strong is your 'family resemblance?'

What would those around you say? What would those in the world say as they observe you? When they hear the words that flow from your lips and watch your actions as you live out the moments of your day, would they say, "What is it about you? I *want* what you *have*!" Or would they just think that you are no different from those who walk this life dead in their sins without Christ and without hope in this world?

Come into My glorious presence often, linger here and be changed. Let the brilliant light of My glory shine upon your soul. Then, as from a mirror, that light will reflect from you into everything you say and do and will, as a simple and natural overflow, touch and impact the world around you and all those you come into contact with…you will shine before them the brilliant reflection of a glorious God, and a heavenly Father who *loves* them!

My little one, when you look to your future, what do you see? Do you see the brightness of My glory, or do you see a dark cloud of fear and uncertainty? What rises in your heart when you look at the days to come?

The hope of heaven, or utter despair?

This morning, I would call you to lift your eyes from the temporal and to place them on the eternal. Lift your eyes from the earthly and set them upon the heavenly. What a great hope you have in Me. I have not only forgiven you and set you free; I have also gone to prepare a place for you, a wonderful place, that where I am you may be also!

Therefore, let hope, glorious hope, fill your heart and mind this morning. I will come again. I will return for you, My bride, and you will live with Me forever in this place where there are no more tears, no more sorrow, no more sickness, no more death. Rejoice!

Rejoice! Let hope rise up once again in your heart!

THE GIFT

Father, I come to You through the cross of Your Son Jesus this morning. Because He took my place on that cross and took all of my sin upon Himself, I come. Because He replaced My sin by covering me with His righteousness, I am worthy in Him through His blood, and I joyfully enter into Your presence!

Yes, come! Come! Come! I have been waiting for you this morning to come to Me. What joy it brings to My heart when My little children appropriate and appreciate the grace I paid so dear a price for and come to Me. My grace is a gift from Me to you that cost Me the precious life of My only Son.

Have you ever given a gift to someone, maybe a child, that cost you much, anticipating the joy that it would bring to the one who would receive? But when you gave it they responded with a casual, "Thanks," or little expression of gratitude whatsoever. Or maybe they received the gift with enthusiasm at first, but when you visited some time later you saw your precious gift pushed to the back of a high shelf, or in a cabinet tucked away with a bunch of meaningless knick-knacks collecting dust, or perhaps at the very bottom of a deep, overflowing bin.

Do you remember the sinking feeling in your heart when you saw the gift that cost you so dearly not being used, being taken for granted, being neglected, being overlooked, ignored, and not appreciated?

My child, use my priceless gift of grace often, for it is by faith that you are saved by this wonderful grace. So come often, leaving your sins and your guilty conscience at the foot of the cross of My Son, allowing Him to wash you in the cleansing flood of His precious blood and dress you in His robes of righteousness, and then enter into the presence of your loving Father clean and unashamed, and abide with Me here before the throne of grace.

"Godliness accompanied by contentment is great gain." I Tim. 6:6

I have you **where** I have you for a **reason**, My dear one.   Is it a comfortable and easy place? No.

But remember that **nothing**—no life circumstance or situation—is ever wasted in My economy.

My child, stop beating at the wind and using all your energy trying to escape this in order to restore the comfort and ease that you long for. Trust Me in it.

Will you turn your eyes to My greater plan for you and for your good? Will you learn while you are here? Will you grow in **this** soil that I have planted you in for **this** season?

Unlike the soil of comfort and ease, there are nutrients to be drawn uniquely from **this** soil of difficulty that will strengthen your roots and make you strong and resilient.

Stop resisting the work I am trying to do. With reckless abandon, let go of **your** desires and **contentedly** embrace **Mine**.

"The Lord directs the steps of the godly. He delights in every detail of their lives." Ps. 37:23

No mistakes, My child...for even your mistakes, your failures, your shortcomings...even the times when you were hurt or grievously sinned against...I have redeemed because you love Me, and I will turn them around for the good. I am the Redeemer. I am the Restorer.

And I have been directing and guiding the steps you have taken...every one! Each day of your life I have been watching over you...every detail of your life precious to Me.

Yes, I delight in you...every moment, every detail...I delight in you. Does it sound strange to your ears that the God who created the entire universe with the word of His mouth, the God who created every star in every galaxy, should care about every tiny detail of your life? I knit you together and formed you in your mother's womb...creating every organ, creating every vein, creating every cell.

My child, I <u>do</u> delight in <u>you</u>, and I <u>love</u> you. Continually commit your way to Me, and I will continue to guide you and direct your steps.

"The sun will not harm you by day, nor the moon by night." Ps. 121:6

*P*icture with Me a small child, frightened and quivering, needing to walk down the stairs and into the darkness of the basement. He turns to his father and says, "Will you hold my hand and come with me?"

My little one, are you frightened and quivering like that child? The future looks dark before you. You can't see where you are going, and you don't know what you might face when you get there.

My child, take My hand and hold tightly to it. Don't be afraid, for I am going with you. I see **all** things clearly, and I will help you not to stumble in the dark. I'll lead you in the safe path. And I know what is ahead of you already and what you will face, and I have already gone before you to fight for you and conquer those things that would rise up against you.

Don't fear the darkness or tremble because you cannot see what lies ahead of you. Rather, cling tightly to Me, and I will lead you safely through.

"Even the darkness will not be dark to you; the night will shine like the noonday for darkness is as light to You, O God." Ps. 139:12
"The sun will no more be your light by day, nor will the brightness of the moon shine on you, for the Lord will be your everlasting light, and your God will be your glory." Isa. 60:19

Many are the joys and pleasures of My presence, if you will but come, My child. Come, and I will renew you here.

There is no other place you can go that will fulfill, bring lasting contentment and joy, give true peace and security to your heart than to rest here in the presence of your Father.

Once you have again tasted the true satisfaction that comes only from abiding with Me, you will be ruined for all else.

Good morning, my sweet Lord. Thank you for always being here when I take the time to come to You. I never find Your arms folded or closed, but rather always open and reaching out to me.   I never find Your eyes turned away and distracted or disinterested, but rather always tenderly gazing my way and piercing through to the very core of my being with the cleansing fire of Your penetrating love. I never find that You've turned and walked away, but rather, just as the Father and the prodigal, You <u>run</u> to meet me. O <u>how I love You, Lord!</u>

Come to Me and abide in Me. For I have heard your anxious cries, and I have seen your fearful thoughts.

Do not be afraid, My child. Rather, choose to trust in Me and *abide* here in My presence.

Come and be still and listen to My voice. For one word which I speak to encourage and strengthen your heart is worth 10,000 others.

Do you lack joy? In My presence is *fullness* of joy. Do you lack peace? I am the Prince of peace. Do you lack hope? I am the God of all hope.

Come into My presence daily and *abide* here with Me, and you will have *no lack*, for I am your all-sufficient source of supply.

"I will instruct you and teach you in the way which you should go; I will counsel you with My eye upon you." Ps. 32:8
"Behold, the eye of the Lord is on those who fear Him, on those who hope for His lovingkindness." Ps. 33:18
"The eyes of the Lord are toward the righteous, and His ears are open to their cry." Ps. 34:15

My beloved, are you afraid to take the next step? Do you fear you are walking blindly and you wonder if I see and am watching, and if it is I that am guiding you according to **My** will?

I see you, My child. My eyes are **ever** upon you. I see that the desire of your heart is to do My will and follow the good path I have set out for your life.

Do not fear, My child, for I will instruct you and teach you in the way which you should go. I **will counsel** you with My eye ever and always upon you.

My child, do you remember the times we used to have together? O how I enjoyed walking with you so closely, and the sweet communion and fellowship we shared together. You were so aware of the reality of My presence, and nothing was as important to you as those times with Me!

I am not calling you to go back to those times, but rather I am calling you on to a new place. I am calling you to a fresh, new place to commune with Me. I am calling you to walk with Me closely throughout your day, constantly aware of My presence with you. I am calling you to make time to listen for My voice as I speak to your heart. I delight in the times when you come to Me in prayer, but you must listen as well as speak.

Do not allow yourself to get caught up with the routine things of everyday, forgetting that I am so close to you... waiting. As you commune with me through your days, you will see them transformed from the mundane and routine to days filled with adventure, joy, and fulfillment. I love you, and I am waiting for you here in this place... so come.

"Your nearness, O God, is my good." Ps. 73:28

"The joy of the Lord is your strength." Neh. 8:10

Whether or not you are exhausted will depend upon where you get your supply. Be exhausted for God, but remember that your supply and strength comes from Him. Make sure that you are trusting Him as the provision for your present as well as your future.

Hosea 2 describes Israel as an unfaithful wife, running after her lovers and forgetting the Lord.

Against this black backdrop of her unfaithfulness, I shine the brilliant light of My mercy and grace toward her. Verses 14-15 say,

"Therefore, behold, I will draw her, and bring her into the wilderness, and speak tenderly to her.
And there I will give her her vineyards and make the Valley of Achor a door of hope.
And she shall sing there as in the days of her youth, as in the day when she came up from the land of Egypt."

Precious…**that's** what you are to Me, My child! **You are precious!**

You have wandered, you have strayed, you have sought the love and affection of others over Me, but My eyes are always upon you…My gaze has never turned away.

Today I am calling you to return to your first love. I desire to restore you. I want you to know Me as the Lover of your soul. I want to be the One that captures your gaze, the One you run to with your struggles and with your joys.

I love you, My child…**dearly** and **deeply**, **eternally** and **unshakably!**

"Therefore, when Mary came where Jesus was, she saw Him, and fell at His feet, saying, 'Lord, if You had been here, my brother would not have died.'
When Jesus therefore saw her weeping, and the Jews who came with her also weeping, He was deeply moved in spirit, and was troubled." John 11:32-33

So many suffering, so many burdened…will you be My hands and feet?

Will you be My arms of comfort to embrace those who are hurting?

Will you weep with those who weep, crying My tears of compassion when others' sorrow is great?

Will you be My hands to help them carry a burden too great for them to bear?

Will your heart break with the things that break Mine?

Will you love them for Me?

And will you implore those who are lost, those who don't know Me, and let them know that I **so loved** the world, so loved **them**, that I gave My precious and only Son to die in their place so that if they will believe in Me they will have life forever in My kingdom?

Will you **touch** them, and **tell** them, for Me?

"Come, everyone who thirsts, come to the waters; and he who has no money, come, buy and eat! Come, buy wine and milk without money and without price. Why do you spend your money for that which is not bread, and your labor for that which does not satisfy?
Listen diligently to me, and eat what is good, and delight yourselves in rich food. Incline your ear, and come to me; hear, that your soul may live." Isa. 55:1-3

My child, are you running after that which the world runs after? Do you hunger after that which the world hungers after—things which are not food, not nourishment?

I have spread a rich feast before you, but you choose to feast on cardboard. It may fill your stomach temporarily, but without any substance of nutrition your spirit will waste away and become emaciated.

Seek after Me with all your heart, **not** after the things of this world. They have no power to fulfill or satisfy. They will fail you miserably. They will leave you spiritually destitute and wanting.

I tell you the truth; Will you **believe** Me...that what I offer you this morning, the riches of My kingdom, the treasure of My precious word, the rewards of living a righteous and God-honoring life out of gratitude that I saved you...what I offer you this morning is the **best!**

I implore you...repent, My **dear child. Turn** and **seek** after that which truly satisfies...seek after Me!

"You have made known to me the path of life; You will fill me with joy in Your presence, with eternal pleasures at Your right hand." Ps. 16:11

My child, what things are you looking to satisfy you and bring you joy?

Are you looking to some of the "harmless" pleasures of this world to fill your longing heart? Beware, for **nothing** is "harmless" if it draws your gaze and your affections away from Me.

Are you looking to people to satisfy this yearning? Only intimacy with **Me** can bring you true contentment, peace, and joy...for only I can fulfill.

Are you so busy doing things <u>for</u> Me (however noble they may be) that you are not pulling away and spending time <u>with</u> Me, which is your highest calling?

Come and let Me refresh your spirit.

Come and let Me speak sweetly and tenderly of My love for you and of My grace towards you. Come and let Me loose once again the springs of joy to well up and spring forth from your spirit and refresh not only you, but also water the weary hearts of others.

The Cross of Grace

Lord, I find myself in this wretched place once again. I have allowed vague feelings of guilt and condemnation to cast their black shadow over my heart.

I feel unworthy to come before You, even though I know in my head that it is not true. I feel as though my feeble prayers fall to the floor the moment they are uttered, although I know in my mind that You hear every one of my prayers and are faithful to answer.

How did I come to be in this place again? How have I let myself come under the burden again of this yoke of condemnation? I know! By not bathing my spirit each morning in Your refreshing stream of grace and allowing that grace to set my heart free.

Oh Lord…I speak to others of Your grace so freely, so convincingly. But how quick I am to forget it myself. I allow clouds of guilt to gradually and subtly roll in and loom so large before me that I can no longer see You. With my view of You obscured, and the devil's cries of 'unworthy' echoing in the chambers of my heart, I seem to sin all the more.

I need to wrap my arms around your cross of grace every morning and not rise from my knees until the truth has shifted from my head to my heart that I am *free indeed!,* until I have cast my eyes upon the cross of my Savior and heard Your voice resounding in my innermost being, You are forgiven…It is <u>finished!</u> You are completely righteous now in the sight of the Father! I must look to the heavens and allow these profound truths to cut my guilty fetters, and instantly my spirit will soar once again to the heights with You.

As the light of Your grace shines upon me, I will be filled with renewed peace, overflowing joy, and hope for the future. And, I would desire with all my heart to serve and obey You and to flee from all sin, not because I am commanded to or obligated to…but out of love and a heart full of gratitude which seeks to please the One who has set me free with His own spilled blood.

The winter has ended. It is springtime once again in my heart.

O Grace…<u>sweet, sweet</u> grace!

"Hope deferred makes the heart sick." Prov. 13:12a

My child, are you downcast and dejected in spirit, and sick in heart this day?

Are you discouraged and disappointed at the lack of growth you see in yourself or others? "Will things ever change?" you cry in despair. Things that you have hoped and prayed for have not yet come to pass as you desired. Loved ones you've been praying for have not yet received My free gift of salvation, and you fear for them.

You look at these unfulfilled desires and have lost all hope that these circumstances will ever change.

I would say to you this morning,

Blessed are those who trust in Me without wavering, even when the evidence around you speaks otherwise.

Blessed are those who **take hold** of the precious promises of My word and **don't let go!**

Stand on them, My child. Stand on them as on a solid rock in the midst of a strong and turbulent sea. Stand on them as solid ground when all around you seems like sinking sand.

Hope in Me once more and in My great and precious promises, for those who hope in the Lord will renew their strength.

"Seek the Lord while He may be found, Call upon Him while He is near.
Let the wicked forsake his way, And the unrighteous man his thoughts;
And let him return to the Lord, And He will have compassion on him;
And to our God,
For He will abundantly pardon." Isa. 55:6-7

Have you drifted in subtle ways from Me, your Savior? Has your heart strayed even the smallest amount from Me, your Lord? Do you lack the excitement and zeal that once filled your heart full at even the thought of being with Me, your Love?

I would say this morning,

Do you remember times past when you felt so far away from Me in your heart? Yet still I was there right beside you all the time, faithfully guiding you back to Me. This morning is no different. You may feel removed in your heart, but I have still never left your side.

I am calling to you now...calling you to return to Me with your whole heart. For I long for the sweet and tender times that we shared. I long to lavish you once again, and to overwhelm you with My presence. I long to meet with you in the quiet place of your heart and to speak softly to you of My love.

So come...come to Me, for even when you have been faithless, I remain faithful...for I cannot deny Myself!

Do the storms of life rage about you on every side? Are you being tossed to and fro on an unmerciful ocean which threatens to tear you apart with every frothing wave that pounds against you?

Do not be afraid, My child, for I am your safe harbor. I am your refuge from the violent storm.

I will not always deliver you out of the tempest, but I will always anchor you firmly and hold you tightly within the storm. Sometimes I will calm the storm, and other times I will comfort you until it passes. Know this, My child...I will never let you go. I have promised to see you through safely to the other side, and I will always be faithful to My promise.

Therefore, although the storm may continue on without, come into the safety of the refuge of My presence, and allow My peace and calm to reign within.

My child, your heart trembles in fear this morning…fear of death. Not physical death, but spiritual. You are afraid that you will fall away, afraid that your feet will slip, that your passion for Me will wane and fade.

But My child, you are focusing on the wrong thing…yourself, instead of Me. Yes, you are weak and frail, you are sinful and unfaithful. But **I** am all sufficient…**all** you need to stand strong!

Fix your eyes on **My** keeping power…the power to keep you from stumbling and falling. Fix your eyes on **My** power to strengthen and sustain you, **My** power to keep you **to the very end** and to present you blameless before My Father!

I'll never give up on you; and I'll never loosen My grip!

"He who has called you is faithful, and He will do it!" I Thess.
5:24

"When the servant of the man of God got up and went out early the next morning, an army with horses and chariots had surrounded the city. 'Oh, my lord, what shall we do?' the servant asked. 'Don't be afraid,' the prophet answered. 'Those who are with us are more than those who are with them.' And Elisha prayed, 'O Lord, open his eyes so he may see.' Then the Lord opened the servant's eyes, and he looked and saw the hills full of horses and chariots of fire all around Elisha." II Kings 6:15-17

My child, which direction are you looking in for answers? Where are you looking for your help to come from? Are you looking in fear toward the invading army which seeks to devour you, or are you looking with a heart of faith to the hills of the Lord?

Only trust and believe, for your redemption draweth nigh. Yes, look to the hills from whence cometh your help, for your deliverance is close at hand!

"And when the scribes of the Pharisees saw that Jesus was eating with the sinners and tax collectors, they began saying to His disciples, 'Why is He eating and drinking with tax collectors and sinners?'
And hearing this, Jesus said to them, 'It is not those who are healthy who need a physician, but those who are sick; I did not come to call the righteous, but sinners.'" Mark 2:16-17

Do you think you have to somehow clean yourself up before you come to Me?   No. I say to you, come just as you are. I did not come to save the perfect, but the wretched…not those who have it all together, but those whose lives have been shattered by sin. I came as a doctor to heal and care for the spiritually sick, not the well.

So, again I say to you, come just as you are. Come with all your failures and mistakes; all your faults and maladies; all your sins, shortcomings, and deficiencies.

It was **you** I came to save…**you** I died to redeem…and **you** that I'm waiting for right now…come just as you are, My child…just as you are…and let Me heal you.

Are you carrying the weight of a heavy burden this morning? Then you are carrying the wrong burden, My child! For My burden is easy and My yoke is light.

Or maybe you are trying to carry the burden in your own strength, rather than in the strength that I provide.

Come humbly before me this morning…find out if this unbearable weight is something which I am calling you to lay down and perhaps never wanted you to take up in the first place, or whether it is the way in which you are carrying it that is burdensome.

I always give the strength and grace for the tasks which I assign

O my Father, hear my cry. Breathe new life into me. Awaken my soul once again.

I have been lulled to sleep, to an inner slumber that I feel like I cannot shake nor escape. But one word from Your lips, Father…one gentle touch from Your loving hand…and I know I shall be roused.

Please come and speak Your tender words to my dull ears now. Please come at this instant and touch my lethargic heart.

This may seem a safe place, a place for the weary soul to rest, but there is no true rest to be had save in Your bosom. This is a dangerous place, indeed, in which I feel I haven't even the strength to feed myself on the meat of Your word…I haven't even strength enough to crawl to the river's edge to drink of Your precious living water.

My unconscious soul says, "Sleep on." No, I dare not! Awake, my soul, within me!…Awake, I say, and behold your Savior! Run to the table which He has spread for you and receive your strength there. Then find true rest in Him alone as you abide in His presence and linger in His embrace.

"But You, O Lord, are a shield about me, my glory and the lifter of my head." Ps. 3:3

Picture with Me a child coming into the presence of his father, head hung low in shame, cowering in unworthiness, expecting rejection and wrath instead of love, forgiveness, and acceptance. The father looks upon his son with a heart filled with compassion, yet sadness as well, because this son, whom he loves so dearly, doubts that love.

Then the father reaches down and gently lifts the head of his beloved child, saying, "Son, look into my eyes and then tell me what you see." The son looks up into the father's eyes and, being overcome by the fullness and depth of the father's love toward him, cries out in joy, "Oh, Father!" and flings his small arms around his neck.

Are you like this child? You have not been walking in the grace and forgiveness purchased for you on the cross. Lingering feelings of unworthiness, guilt, and shame hang over you instead of the favor and pleasure of your heavenly Father. Although you desire to come into My presence, you come with head hung low, expecting rejection and wrath instead of love and forgiveness.

But I would reach down this morning and gently lift your head, saying,

My child, look into My eyes and tell Me what you see. Let your heart be overwhelmed by the fullness and depth of My love for you which you see there.

Cry out in joy this morning, sing a new song from the depths of your heart, proclaim My goodness, and praise Me with a loud voice...for you are loved dearly by Me, My child.

I believe that God, who spoke the very universe into existence by the power of His word, would speak some very specific words to the hearts of some this morning.

Be comforted, My people.

Though it seems right now that all is against you…I am for you.

When all around you, strife and trouble rise, I **speak** peace—peace to your heart, peace to your soul—receive it now.

When before you loom mountains insurmountable, I **speak** strength and courage—receive it now, and you will mount up, as I have declared in My word, on wings like eagles.

When despair comes in like a cloud, I speak hope—receive it now.

I am all you need in every trial.

Receive from Me the peace, strength, courage, and hope that I freely give you now.

"And you will seek Me and find Me, when you search for Me with all your heart." Jer. 29:13

If you desire to <u>know </u>Me, you must earnestly seek Me. And as you <u>seek</u> Me, I will draw near to you. And I will come to you and overwhelm you with My presence as I loose the bonds of self that have kept you bound.

I will cleanse your guilty conscience so that you may, once again, walk in the joy of forgiving grace. I will restore your soul and lead you beside quiet streams of refreshing.

O, I yearn for you to come. For I long to set you free and to draw you near to me; to speak tenderly to you of My redeeming love; to birth new joy, hope, and faith into your heart with one word from My lips.

So come near and rest your head on My bosom. Draw near and enter My rest.

"And you will be called by a new name, which the mouth of the Lord will designate. You will also be a crown of beauty in the hand of the Lord, and a royal diadem in the hand of your God. It will no longer be said to you, 'Forsaken,' nor to your land will it any longer be said, 'Desolate.' But you will be called, 'My delight is in her,'...for the Lord delights in you." Isa. 62:2b-4

My child, I *do delight* in you. Right now you are even thinking, "This word is for everyone else," but you are unable to receive it into your own heart. No, My child, I speak to **you** this morning...I delight in **you**! Why have you believed the lies of the enemy? Why do you listen to the words of the deceiver and enemy of your soul rather than to the Lover of your soul? Hear My words to you this morning again, and allow them to penetrate to the very core of your being...

I delight in **you!**

My child,

Is My grace still amazing to you, or have your ears become dull to the Gospel because you have heard it over and over again, maybe even from the time you were young? Has your heart become unaffected by its wonderful, glorious truth? When you hear the Gospel recounted, do you respond in your heart with, "Oh yes, I already know that," or does your heart cry out…

"Oh God, I was a sinner bounding headlong for hell. Thank you for saving me, not based on any good works that I've done or anything that was good in me. No, it was simply because it pleased You to call me and draw me. It was Your good will and desire to crush Your perfect and precious Son so that You could adopt this wretch as Your very own child—You poured out all Your wrath upon Him who didn't deserve it so that You could pour out Your complete and total favor on me who didn't deserve it. You rejected Him, the Perfect One who loved You, so that You could love me, the guilty and vile one who was in complete rebellion against You.

And now, because of the exchange that took place that day on the cross, You see me clothed in the righteousness and perfectness of Your Son, so now I can come to You, right into Your very presence, freely and confidently in Jesus' name and covered with His righteousness that bought my access to You!"

Child, is My grace still amazing?

"O Israel, the Lord who created you says, 'Do not be afraid, for I have ransomed you. I have called you by name; you are mine.'" Isa. 43:1

O how precious you are to Me. You are a priceless treasure, a trophy of My grace on display for a dying, searching world.

I say to you again, **you** are **precious** to Me. Don't be afraid as you encounter various trials. I have not abandoned you to face your struggles alone. How could I ever leave the one I gave everything to redeem? How could I ever walk away from the child in whom I so delight?

No, I will not forsake you, but rather will give you the strength that you need to overcome the hardships you now face.

And know that, as a trophy of My grace, you will shine forth My glory even more brilliantly when you find yourself up against the dark backdrop of troubled and uncertain times, but yet in the midst of them your lips continue to praise Me and sing of My faithfulness and goodness. And as you, in the face of difficulty, allow the steady, unwavering brilliance of your trust in Me to radiate, many hearts will be touched, and many lives brought closer to the source of that light.

My child, do you feel like you have failed your family in some way, or that you are not the strong yet loving and compassionate parent to your children that I have called you to be?

I would ask you this morning, am I not greater than your mistakes? I am the Mighty Restorer. I will redeem the days, months, years, and perhaps even decades, as you press into My presence and let Me change you and form you into My image: a parent who is strong, yet filled with compassion, love, and tenderness for His precious children and motivates them by His glorious grace to obey and follow the good path that leads to life.

My child, humble yourself this day and repent, but then look back no longer. Instead, look forward and trust in My redemptive power to change, heal, and to restore.

Behold, I am doing a new thing. Even now it springs forth. And be not afraid, for as I lead you into places unknown, I will hold you securely and tenderly in My hand.

Although I lead you into strange waters, I will never, ever forsake or abandon you. And I will never lead you to a place where My grace cannot sustain you.

Treasure the moments of intimacy that come as you cling to Me in the unknown. And trust Me that although it is unclear to you where you are headed, I see all things clearly, and I am the One who is holding you by the hand and leading you in a good way.

"Behold, I go forward, but He is not there, and backward, but I cannot perceive Him; when He acts on the left, I cannot behold Him; when He turns on the right, I cannot see Him. But He knows the way I take; when He has tried me, I shall come forth as gold. My foot has held fast to His path; I have kept His way and not turned aside. I have not departed from the command of His lips; I have treasured the words of His mouth more than my necessary food." Job 23:8-12

My child, I am so proud of you and the way that you are walking through your afflictions with a desire to bring glory to Me.

Although you don't see My hand at work, you have trusted Me, knowing that **I am** with you regardless of your feelings.

And **yes, I do know** the way that you take and the struggles you bear. This is actually a path I have destined for you, not to crush you, but to strengthen you…not to cause you to stumble, but to raise you up!

Continue to honor Me in the midst of the struggles, clinging tightly to My hand, even though you may not feel it within your own. Continue to treasure My words in your heart, for they will be to you life, and a well of strength which you can draw from.

And, My precious child, I **will** bring you forth as gold!

"Draw near to God and He will draw near to you." Jas. 4:8
"Perfect love casts out all fear." I John 4:18

Why do you hesitate to draw near to Me? Why do you shrink back from My presence?

Child, please know that the hand that I am stretching out to you this morning reaches out not to condemn or punish you, but rather in tender affection to draw you to Myself. My arms long to embrace you. My heart aches to show you My love toward you afresh…My perfect love for you which never changes, never wanes.

Cast off all fear and condemnation which would hold you back and keep you from Me at arm's length. Come boldly and without inhibition as a young child runs into the waiting arms of his or her father. For so I wait for you.

"Consider it all joy, my brethren, when you encounter various trials, knowing that the testing of your faith produces endurance." Jas. 1:2-3

My child, are you walking in joy through your current trials? You could if you would realize and embrace this truth: that these trials will grow you and make you **stronger** if you stand in faith and keep your eyes fixed on Me.

Don't doubt…trust Me!

Don't fear…rely on Me!

Don't give up…lean on Me for the strength you need, for I will get you through this and you will overcome!

These obstacles are opportunities to show forth My glory and strength in your life, and to strengthen your faith in an Almighty God who can do the impossible and in a heavenly Father who **loves** you so much!!

"From [Christ] the whole body, joined and held together by every supporting ligament, grows and builds itself up in love, as each part does its work." Eph. 4:16

Make A Difference:

Change A Life…Change Your World!

How??? By submitting the gifts and talents which I have given you every morning back to Me.

Is the consistent posture, attitude, and desire of your heart to "get a blessing", or to be used by Me to "be a blessing" in the lives of others? Amazingly, it is when you purpose in your heart to bless others that you yourself are blessed the most!

Is the prayer of your heart, "Lord, how can You use the gifts and talents You have given me to bless others today in Your Name?" Have I given you the gift of prophecy? Then pray, "Lord, what do You want to speak to Your people this day?" Have I given you the gift of hospitality? Then pray, "Lord, who can I bless today by bringing them into my home, and ministering to them through physical food and spiritual fellowship?" Have I given you the gift of evangelism? Than pray, "Lord, would You send me an opportunity this day to share Your love as demonstrated in the cross of Christ with someone who is still lost in their sins?"

Have I given you the gift of music, writing, encouragement, mercy, helps, compassion,…? Then come before Me this morning and lay them down again at My feet and ask Me how you can use them today for My glory and honor to touch the heart and life of another, and to further My kingdom. I *delight* to answer prayers like these!

Just think for a minute about what the church, and the world, would look like if all My children did this…a lot different!!!

"Come now, let us reason together, says the Lord; though your sins are like scarlet, they shall be as white as snow; though they are red like crimson, they shall become like wool." Isa. 1:18

I believe that this is a cry from the heart of God this morning…that there are some who are uncertain of their standing before Him, who are unsure whether they are still under the judgment and wrath of God, or whether they have truly been forgiven and crossed over from death into life.

But hear the heart of the Savior this morning…He wants you to know that you know that you know, so that when the storms of life come, this will be the anchor of your soul that keeps you from being swept away.

This morning, are you cowering before a perfect and righteous Judge, or coming to the open arms of a loving Father?

He wants you to **know** that His grace covers you this morning…that you have been freely and completely forgiven, so that you have full assurance of faith that you can freely come into His presence, not in your sin as an object of His wrath…but as a *son* or *daughter*.

I believe the Lord gave me a picture in my mind this morning of a great, beautiful body of water. And in this body of water, there were many people washing, playing, and simply enjoying the cool refreshment.

Yet, there were others remaining at the edge of the waters. They were tired, hot, and weary. But they were merely looking on and watching the others, not entering into the refreshing waters themselves.

I believe the Lord would say,

My child, this body of water represents My life-giving Holy Spirit. And while many are entering into and enjoying the fullness of My presence, you are lingering at the water's edge and looking on.

Do not be content or satisfied to just sit back and look on this morning. Enter in for yourself…hold nothing back! Wade into the deep waters of My presence and let Me wash you and refresh you.

Do not be content or satisfied to just simply dip your big toe in. Come in deeper…be immersed in My life-giving waters…come in deeper, My child! For I have so much more for you!

Come in deeper this morning, My child!

I heard the gentle whisper in my spirit, very quiet. The Lord spoke softly asking me to come...so soft was His still, small voice that I almost missed it.

The flesh is such a wicked, evil, vile thing that loathes the presence of the Lord. But I am glad I stopped, and came, and am... Refreshment, true refreshment, lies only here...in the sweet presence.

Entertainment seeks to numb us from our painful reality...from the heart crying within our breast because it desperately needs to be filled by Him...from our dissatisfaction with the emptiness and futility of life...from the senselessness and insanity that we observe all around us...from the insecurity of a life in which we can count on nothing, rely on nothing, put our faith in nothing...for everything changes-- there is no constant in life and no stability or security apart from Him. For He alone is the Unchangeable, Immutable, Almighty One...the Sovereign God!

Our lives must rest securely on this Rock or we will forever find ourselves tossed to and fro on the tumultuous waves of life. If we anchor our lives on the Rock, the waves may still swell up high around us, but He will be our stay. I am secure in the largeness of the Hand that holds so tightly to mine--and has promised to never release its grip!

Come Up Higher

Lord, I want to emanate the sweet aroma of the fragrance of Christ to others.

This, My child, can only happen if you live your life nearer to Me, coming often to spend time with Me, resting your weary head on the breast of the One who loves you.

Lord, I don't want to be the same person I have been, stale and stagnating, reeking with the stench of the world instead of the lovely perfume of Your grace and presence. I want to forever be changed, from glory to glory, from having been with You.

Come up higher, My child. Don't be content to merely touch the hem of My garment and then return to the world. My arms wait to embrace you.

Come up higher and walk this life hand in hand with Me. Only then will others recognize that you have been with the Savior, and the aroma of My sweet grace and forgiveness will draw many, not to you, but through you to Me.

"By his divine power, God has given us everything we need for living a godly life." 2 Pet. 1:3 (NLT)

'The weight is too great for me, the burden too heavy, the task too difficult!' you exclaim. You are trying to hold things together, trying to keep up a good face when inside you are crying and overwhelmed.

Don't give up, My child…persevere! For I will give you all that you need, I will equip you for that to which I've called you, and I will strengthen you.

But let go of trying to do this in your own strength. Instead, lean on Me and the strength I have promised to provide. For I have given you all that you need in Me!

"I will sing of the lovingkindness of the Lord forever; to all generations I will make known Your faithfulness with my mouth. And the heavens will praise Your wonders, O Lord, and Your faithfulness also in the assembly of the holy ones. O Lord God of hosts, who is like You, O mighty Lord? Your faithfulness also surrounds You." Ps. 89:1,5 (NAS)

Faithful, My child…I have been faithful for all these years. Today I would encourage you to look back upon the many blessings I have lavished upon you, the many miracles I have done in your life, the many ways My hand has moved in days past to deliver you, strengthen you, sustain you, uphold you.

My child, let these memories of My faithfulness be the fuel to ignite the fire of your present trust and hope… may faith rise up in your spirit that, just as so many times before, I will be faithful, both now and in the days and years to come.

You are My child…My precious, precious child. I love you just as much now as I did when you first answered My call and came to Me, and received My gift of salvation. I love you just as much now as I did when you recommitted your life back into My hands after your season of wandering. When you returned, you were welcomed with joy by My outstretched arms of grace. I love you just as much now as I did in any of the sweetest times of communion and tender intimacy we have shared together in the past…the many times you lingered quietly and allowed My presence to overwhelm you, the times you came and received My comfort in moments of sorrow, the many times of joy we shared.

I am still the same, and My love toward you remains unchanged. Find joy and peace in the revelation of this truth upon your spirit…You are still My precious, precious child.

As you come into My presence every morning and allow Me to remind you of My undying love for you, I will give you the strength that you need for that day and all that it will bring. However, just as with the manna which I sent My people in the wilderness, I do not give tomorrow's strength today. You will find that the grace which you received in your time with Me yesterday is no longer able to sustain you today.

My mercies and My abundant grace are new every morning for you to gather…before the fiery trials and cares of the world and pressures of the day rise. Just as the blistering noon sun burned off the manna which still lay ungathered by the Israelites upon the desert floor, the fiery trials, the cares of the world, and the pressures of the day can rise and burn off My provision of grace which lies ungathered by you.

So, come and gather this morning of the bread of heaven. And I will satisfy and sustain you with My abundant grace.

"For I know the plans I have for you," says the LORD. "They are plans for good and not for disaster, to give you a future and a <u>hope</u>." Jer. 29:11 (NLT)

Yes…I am the God of all hope. My child, in what state do you find yourself this morning?

Are you weary and discouraged? Place your hope in Me and in the precious, unwavering promises of My word.

Do you feel condemned? Put your hope in My forgiveness and in My unfailing, unconditional love toward you. Put your

hope in My sweet grace…free, undeserved, and unearned.

Have you been misjudged or falsely accused? Put your hope in Me, My child, for I am your defense, and your vindication is from Me. I am the Aid that will rush to your side in defense and strengthen you, hold you up, and encourage your heart.

Do you fear what the future holds?

Hope in the fact that I, the One who loves you beyond what you can comprehend, hold your future in My hands. Hope in the promise that I have made not to place upon you more than you can bear. Hope in the fact that I have <u>promised</u> to <u>sustain</u> you through the most difficult of trials.

Hope in My promise to go before you and behind you, and to walk this road beside you and hold you up by My hand. Hope in Me.

"Behold, I go forward but He is not there, and backward, but I cannot perceive Him; When He acts on the left, I cannot behold Him; He turns on the right, I cannot see Him. But He knows the way I take." Job 23:8-10a (NAS)

My beloved, you are like a child groping blindly in the dark, unsure of where to place your feet, afraid of stumbling and falling, not sure of what lies before you hidden from view by darkness, feeling as if you are walking this frightening path alone.

But, dear one, I am leading you, even when you are unaware of My presence. Not only do I know the way that you take, I go before you, walk beside you, and encompass you on every side. I am with you.

All of your days are known by Me, and I am **fully present** in each one, even the days ahead of you that you have yet to live out, to carry you when your strength fails, to walk beside you as your helper and friend.

I **am** with you *all* of your days…

"Come, everyone who thirsts, come to the waters; and he who has no money, come, buy and eat!
Come; buy wine and milk without money and without price.
Why do you spend your money for that which is not bread, and your labor for that which does not satisfy?
Listen diligently to Me, and eat what is good, and delight yourselves in rich food." Isa. 55:1-2

See here, My child! I have spread before you today a bountiful table filled with delights. I call you to come…come to the table that I have prepared for you and partake freely of My rich feast.

But I would say to you, come hungry. Do not fill yourself with the empty, vain, hollow offerings of this world. If you have indulged yourself in the temporary, fleeting pleasures this world has to offer, your appetite will be spoiled for the things of God.

And know that I do not give sparingly, but I call you to come and eat your fill of My goodness, My mercy, My grace, and My love. Come and drink in of the sweetness of My presence and partake of that which alone can truly satisfy your soul, give you joy overflowing, give you strength for the day, and fill your heart with peace…such peace.

Come and feast upon Me!

"And the word of God came to Jeremiah, saying, 'Arise, and go down to the potter's house, and there I will let you hear My words.' So I went down to the potter's house, and there he was working at his wheel. And the vessel he was making of clay was spoiled in the potter's hand, and he reworked it into another vessel, as it seemed good to the potter to do." Jer. 18:1-4

My child, can I not do with you as the potter had done? Just like the clay in the hand of the potter, so you are in My hand.

You see your life as that spoiled clay, as that ruined vessel. You thought you knew what shape your life should take, but now things are different than you had planned or imagined, and you are disillusioned and discouraged.

But, I would say to you this morning, I am reworking the clay. I am reforming you, reshaping you, refining you, and remaking you into a vessel of honor, a vessel fit for noble use, to be used for noble purposes.

It is not apparent to you now exactly what I am making of you, or all that I am doing in your life. But you must trust the skillful hands and loving touch of the Potter, and yield yourself to them.

And when the vessel is finished, you will look back and exclaim, "What a wonderful work God has done!"

"Bless the Lord, O my soul, and forget not all His benefits, who forgives all your iniquity, who heals all your diseases; who redeems your life from the pit,…The Lord is merciful and gracious, slow to anger and abounding in steadfast love…He does not deal with us according to our sins, nor repay us according to our iniquities. For as high as the heavens are above the earth, so great is His steadfast love toward those who fear Him; as far as the east is from the west, so far does He remove our transgressions from us. As a father shows compassion to His children, so the Lord shows compassion to those who fear Him." Ps. 103:2-13

Dear child, why are you downcast this morning? Why is your soul in turmoil within you? Could it be that you have forgotten some of My benefits?

Draw near and come to the cross even now and let Me remind you that I have forgiven all your iniquity and washed away all of your sin. There is no stain upon you now.

Come to the cross and remember that I am the One who redeemed your life from the pit. When you wandered and went astray, I earnestly sought you. And when you turned your heart once again toward home, I ran to meet you and embraced you as the father did the prodigal son.

Come to the cross and see again, as you look upon the suffering of My Son, the height and the depth of My great compassion, mercy, and amazing love toward you. Remember, though your sins were as scarlet, now they are whiter than snow.

Remind yourself often of these truths.

"Six days before the Passover, Jesus came to Bethany, where Lazarus was, whom Jesus had raised from the dead. So they gave a dinner for Him there. Martha served, and Lazarus was one of those reclining with Him at the table.

Mary therefore took a pound of expensive ointment made from pure nard, and anointed the feet of Jesus and wiped His feet with her hair. The house was filled with the fragrance of the perfume." John 12:1-3

Mary, out of her heart overflowing with gratitude for all I had done for her, could not keep herself back from performing this lavish display of adoration and love toward Me. She held nothing back, not even her most precious possession, from her Savior.

My child, have I not done as much for you? When you were lost, I sought after you. When you were blind, I opened your eyes to see My love for you and My great salvation.

What is the thing that is precious to your heart this morning?

What is the thing in your life that you are maybe holding onto and keeping back from Me?

My child, out of the gratefulness of your heart, will you now pour it out at My feet as an offering of extravagant love, of radical, passionate devotion? I tell you the truth, it will mean as much to Me as that costly, sweet perfume and will be a pleasing, fragrant sacrifice that will ascend before the very throne of God.

"For you shall go out in joy and be led forth in peace." Isa. 55:12

My child, what is the source of your joy this morning? If it is Me, it cannot be shaken. But if it is the temporary happiness of the things of this world, it will be short-lived and will leave you empty and despairing.

Seek after the lasting joy that only I can give and that no man can take away from you. Cry out to Me as the psalmist did, "Restore to me the joy of your salvation!" Ps. 51:12a

"How can I come to You, O God?" you cry out in your heart this morning. "I am broken, sick, poor, a sinner, a failure. I am a pot full of cracks, unusable, a vessel for dishonor."

But hear what the Lord would speak to you this day in Romans 9:22-24a:

"What if God, although willing to demonstrate His wrath and to make His power known, endured with much patience vessels of wrath prepared for destruction?

And He did so in order that He might make known the riches of His glory upon vessels of mercy, which He prepared beforehand for glory, even us, whom He also called…"

My child, I will take your sins, your failures, your mistakes, your shortcomings, your incompetencies… and I will *redeem* them *all*, transforming them from worthless and dishonorable and shameful, into things of beauty.

Lay them at My feet and watch Me turn them all into something beautiful that I will use to show forth My glory…

I *will* create *beauty* from the ashes of your life!

"For My thoughts are not your thoughts, neither are your ways My ways, declares the Lord.
For as the heavens are higher than the earth, so are My ways higher than your ways and My thoughts than your thoughts."
Isa. 55:8

My child, you don't understand what I am doing in your life. You can't see clearly nor comprehend the workings of My hand.

But I would ask you one question this morning…Do you <u>trust</u> Me? You trusted Me as your Savior, now do you trust Me as your Provider…as your Deliverer?

I ask you again this morning…Do you <u>trust</u> Me? True trust comes in when things look bleakest yet you choose to stand firm in the belief that I am the Almighty God who is able to save <u>and</u> that I love you <u>dearly</u> and am <u>for</u> you and will work all things together for My glory and for your good.

Look to the solution, not to the problem. Keep your eyes on <u>Me</u>, not on your circumstances.

I ask you again…Do you trust Me this morning with an unwavering faith?

<u>Do</u> you <u>trust</u> Me?

"'Though the mountains be shaken and the hills be removed yet My unfailing love for you will not be shaken, nor My covenant of peace be removed,' says the Lord, who has compassion on you." Isa. 54:10 (NIV)

Are you facing circumstances that you never thought you would have to face?

My dear one, when it seems like the very earth under your feet is giving way…I've got you.

I will be the rock beneath you when things are shaking, so you can stand firm. And I will be the anchor to hold you steady against the crashing waves…I've got you.

You feel like your circumstances are careening out of control, but they are **never** out of **My** control. You are not in some bottomless 'freefall'—you are being held in the hands of your loving Father.

I will hold you tight and will carry you securely and lovingly in My arms…

I've got you

"Thus says the Lord:
'[They] found grace in the wilderness. When Israel sought for
rest, the Lord appeared to him from far away. I have loved you
with an everlasting love; therefore I have continued My
faithfulness to you. Again I will build you, and you shall be
built…With weeping they shall come, and with cries for mercy I
will lead them back. I will make them walk by brooks of water,
in a straight path in which they shall not stumble, and they
shall be radiant over the goodness of the Lord…and they shall
languish no more.
Then shall the young women rejoice in the dance, and the
young men and the old shall be merry. I will turn their
mourning into joy; I will comfort them, and give them gladness
for sorrow…And I will pour out of My abundance, and My
people shall be satisfied with My goodness,' declares the Lord."
Jer. 31:2-4, 9, 13, 14b

My dear child, I have seen your tears. I have wept with you when you wept. In your pain, run to Me, for I am the One who comforts, heals, and restores. And I will heal you. Give your broken heart to Me, and let Me heal it as only I can. I will turn your mourning into joy and your sorrow into gladness, your despair into bright hope. And your heart will once again sing over the goodness of your Lord.

My child, you find yourself shocked and discouraged at the depravity of your heart and the sin that resides there. Your heart condemns you unceasingly. But I am not shocked at your sin. It grieves My heart when you disobey Me because I know that the end of disobedience and sin is death…but I am not shocked nor surprised by it.

I knew before the beginning of time that you were going to commit that very sin. I saw it being acted out, no matter how depraved it may be, before I went to the cross in your place. And despite that sin, I chose you, and despite that sin, I called you to be My precious child.

Now, in light of this amazing grace and mercy, and with all the *power* I *supply*, I call you to lay aside the sin which so easily entangles. For only My Spirit can change your heart and break the chains of the sin that binds you. So come to Me with full assurance of faith that I can, and will, help you overcome the sin that enslaves you, whose hold you are desperate to break, in order that you may run this race unfettered for the glory of your loving Father!

"The Lord is merciful and gracious, slow to anger, and abounding in steadfast love...
He does not deal with us as our sins deserve, nor does He repay us according to our iniquities. For as high as the heavens are above the earth, so great is His steadfast love toward those who fear Him; as far as the east is from the west, so far does He remove our transgressions from us.
As a father shows compassion to his children, so the Lord shows compassion to those who fear Him.
For He knows our frame; He remembers that we are dust." Ps. 103:8-14

My child, are you more aware of My steadfast love, compassion, and forgiveness this morning, or do you feel condemned before Me by the weight of your sin and the amount of your shortcomings?

I want you to know this morning that it is your own heart which condemns you, not Me. Not only do I not condemn you, but I love you deeply with a love that does not change even when you fall short.

I also want you to remember this morning that I have not left you alone in your battle against sin. I have sent you My Holy Spirit as your helper, not only to shine My light on the sin of your heart in order to reveal it to you, but then to draw alongside to help you conquer it. He will give you both the willingness and the power to change.

Be assured this morning of My steadfast love toward you despite your failings. And be assured of the bountiful help I have sent you, and draw upon it!

"I shall remember the deeds of the Lord; surely I will remember Thy wonders of old, I will meditate on all Thy work, and muse on Thy deeds." Ps. 77:11-12

Oh My child, sometimes in the midst of the storm you forget how many other times I have brought you safely to harbor...you forget in times of trouble how many times I have rescued and delivered you in days gone by. You forget My goodness and faithfulness that I have so vividly and lovingly demonstrated and displayed throughout your life, and faith gives way to fear as your circumstances loom larger in your eyes than your God.

Have I not given you every reason to trust Me? Have I not shown you time and again that I am faithful and that I love you?

This morning, will you choose to say with the Psalmist, "But as for me, I trust in You, O Lord. I say, 'You are my God! My times are in Thy hand.'" Ps. 31:14-15a? (NAS)

"The steps of a man are established by the Lord, when He delights in his way; though he falls, he shall not be cast headlong, for the Lord upholds his hand." Ps.37:23-24

Yes, My child, you have made some mistakes in your past. But I am the great Redeemer…not only the Redeemer of your soul, but also the Redeemer of your failures, the Redeemer of your shortcomings, the Redeemer of your mistakes.

What joy and delight I have in taking these things that the enemy meant to stumble you with or to even destroy you with, and turning them around for My glory and your good.

'But Lord,' you say, 'could you possibly bring any good out of this failure?' Yes, My child…even *that one.*

Any failure or mistake brought to the foot of the cross and laid humbly before Me can be washed in My blood and transformed into a trophy of My grace. Bring them all now and place them at My feet, and stand amazed at the glorious thing I can create from them!

"Commit your way to the Lord. Trust also in Him, and He will do it." Ps. 37:5

My child, spend extended time in My presence, and let Me align **your** goals with **mine**.

Then you can come **boldly** before My throne of grace and pray with confidence, knowing that you are setting your vision on, and putting your hand to, that which **I** desire to do in and through your life.

Don't be discouraged when My plans seem delayed. Trust in the waiting that in due time, in My time, I will bring forth My will in your life. This is nothing you must contrive or force to happen.

As you walk forward step by step in the way that I lead you, trust Me to open the doors I want opened and to close firmly those that are not My best for you.

On your knees I will lead you, and **I will** accomplish all that concerns you!

"'And it will come about in that day,' declares the Lord, 'that you will call Me Ishi (meaning 'my husband') and will no longer call Me Baali (meaning 'my master').'" Hos. 2:16

Dear one, you long to belong, long to be accepted and treasured by another, long to be loved unconditionally just for who you are.

I want you to know this morning, beloved, that you are **mine**:

…not as a slave, but as a child who is the apple of My eye and brings great delight and joy to My heart as your Father.

…not as a servant, but as a bride, beautiful and altogether lovely in the eyes of her groom.

My beloved, you **belong** to **Me**.

"The Lord your God is in your midst, a victorious warrior. He will exult over you with joy, He will be quiet in His love, He will rejoice over you with shouts of joy!" Zeph. 3:17 (NAS)

"[God] will yet fill your mouth with laughter and your lips with shouts of joy." Job 8:21

My child, what sorrow has overtaken you? What sadness has darkened your soul?

You feel that none can understand what you are going through...but I can. I am a Man of Sorrows, and am very well acquainted with the bitterness of grief. And I call you to come and pour out your burdens upon Me, for I am able to bear what you cannot.

Lean on Me through this time and find solace and comfort in the arms of the One who truly understands better than any other, and the only One who can bring healing to the wounds of your heart.

And yes, I <u>will</u> fill your mouth with laughter once again, and your lips will shout with joy of My goodness and faithfulness. Let this bring hope to your heart.

"Nevertheless, I am continually with Thee; Thou hast taken hold of my right hand. With Thy counsel Thou wilt guide me, and afterward receive me to glory." Ps. 73:23-24 (NAS)

My child, rejoice not only in My power to *save* you, but also in My power to *keep* you to the end!

You are so afraid of *falling*, that it is hindering your *walk* with Me.

My dear one, do not let your heart be filled with fear, but rather *trust* in *Me*—not in your own willpower and ability to stand strong—for I *will see* you through and bring you into My glory. I've got you, My child…I've *got* you!

And, the mistakes you've made along the way, those things that have caused you heartache and shame…bring them to Me, lay them down at My feet and let me *redeem* them and *restore* you—for I *will*…I *will*!

Trust Me to keep you from falling and to present you blameless on the day you stand before My throne!!

"Blessed is the man who walks not in the counsel of the wicked, nor stands in the way of sinners, nor sits in the seat of scoffers; but his delight is in the law of the Lord, and on his law he meditates day and night. And he shall be like a tree, planted by streams of water, that yields its fruit in its season, and its leaf does not wither. In all that he does, he prospers." Ps. 1:1-3

Behold, I am doing a new thing...even now it springs forth. I am bringing you into a <u>new </u>season in your life, a time of refreshing and new growth...springtime.

And you <u>will</u> be that tree of which the Psalmist spoke. And I will send the spring rains of my Spirit to water you, and you will draw your nourishment from the rich soil of my word.

I will cause your roots to go down deep; and when the storms of life come, your faith will not be uprooted, but you will be able to stand firm.

And your branches will bud once again; then will you bear abundant fruit. And others will come under the shelter of your boughs, and will enjoy sweet rest in the refreshing shade given by your lush foliage, and will receive nourishment from the fruit you bear.

I am bringing you into this new season of rich, abundant life in Me, so that you may bring life to others.

"May the God of hope fill you with all joy and <u>peace as you trust in Him</u>, so that you may <u>overflow</u> with <u>hope</u> by the power of the Holy Spirit." Rom. 15:13

What dream have I placed in your heart? What thing have I spoken to your heart in secret? Have you given up hope; have you lost the vision? I have not…

For I created you to do good works which I prepared for you before the beginning of time, that you should walk in them. I have a wonderful plan for your life, birthed at the cross of your salvation.

Haven't I said in Jeremiah, 'For I know the plans that I have for you, declares the Lord, plans for good and not for evil, to give you a future and a <u>hope</u>?'

Therefore, pray earnestly, believing in faith that I can do in you and through you what seems to you to be impossible. Keep your eyes on Me, and put your hand to the plow, and allow Me to unfold the vision that I have for your life into reality in due season.

"The plans of the Lord stand firm forever, the purposes of His heart through all generations." Ps. 33:11

"Rejoice in the Lord always, again I say, Rejoice!" Phil. 4:4

My child, are you choosing to be joyful this morning? Is your heart happy in God? Are you delighting and gladdening yourself in Me?

I am calling you this morning to remember; and in remembering, to rejoice.

Remember that because of My sacrifice, now your sins are no longer counted against you.

Rejoice that I called you by name to be My own, and that now your name is written in My Book of Life.

Let your heart be *glad* as you remember the depths of My love for you, and the lavishness of My grace and mercy toward you.

Delight in the fact that My love for you will *never change*; it is *infinite* and *constant*, *not* dependent upon your goodness or your obedience, but *forever made firm* by the righteousness of My Son which covers you.

Let your heart break forth and sing for joy this morning!

Remember…and choose joy!

Our citizenship is in heaven. And we eagerly await a Savior from there, the Lord Jesus Christ, who, by the power that enables Him to bring everything under His control, will transform our lowly bodies so that they will be like His glorious body.
Therefore, my brothers…that is how you should stand firm in the Lord, dear friends." Phil. 3:20-4:1

Have you forgotten that My return is close at hand? Have you lost sight of the fact that I am coming back *for you*, My precious son, and *for you*, My beloved daughter?

If you knew that I was coming back tomorrow, how would that knowledge affect you today?

Live in light of My imminent return! *Eagerly* await your Savior! Cling to this promise; hold fast to this hope that is within you. For yes, My return is close at hand. And you shall be with

Me…and you shall be *changed*!

"I will go before you and make the rough places smooth; I will shatter the doors of bronze, and cut through their iron bars. And I will give you the treasures of darkness and hidden wealth of secret places in order that you may know that it is I, the Lord, the God of Israel, who calls you by your name." Isa. 45:2-3

My dear one, are you struggling in the area of your finances right now?

I call you to continue to be faithful and diligent to do what I've called you to do—work heartily as unto Me—and trust Me to provide all that you have need of.

Do not fear, nor be anxious, saying, 'Does the Lord know my great need? Does my heavenly Father even hear my cries for help and see my dire situation?'

Dear child, I not only see your need, I not only hear your cry, but I have also already planned the provision you need.

And, My beloved, it will be glorious to behold, and an amazing answer to your prayers. For I will bring your provision from the hidden wealth of secret places, not from any of the places, ways, or means that you might anticipate, so that you will know that your provision is from **My** hand, and you will **know** that I, your Father, love you and will provide **every need you face!**

"What is man, that you are mindful of him, or the son of man, that you care for him?" Ps. 8:4

It is truly a divine paradox: I created you, and you are completely dependent upon Me. Even your every breath comes from Me.

Yet, frail and weak as you are, I have chosen you to work My will and to carry forth My purposes in this world.

Will you humbly set your hand to what I am doing? Humbly, because you realize that you can do nothing of yourself…it's all from Me.

Will you fervently be about your Father's business?

Fervently, because the days are short and there is much left to do. Your life is but a breath…merely a vapor, and then it is gone. Will you make it count for eternity? Will you leave a lasting impact in this world by emptying yourself of self, and allowing Me to use you to touch the hearts of others?

I desire to fill up the vessel of your life with the life-giving water of My Holy Spirit, then to use you to fill the empty cups of so many broken lives, so many shattered, hurting people.

So then, I ask you the question again: Will you humbly and fervently be about your Father's business?

"Blessed is he whose transgressions are forgiven, whose sins are covered. Blessed is the man whose sin the Lord does not count against him." Ps. 32:1-2

Are you coming to Me based on your own merits this morning, or on the righteous merits of My Son?

Or, are you shrinking back because you know that your own merits fall pitifully short of the holiness I require?

I tell you to come by way of the cross, allowing the blood of Jesus to wash and cleanse your guilty conscience.

Come boldly, come with overflowing joy, knowing that your sins have been forgiven, and that I completely accept you as My own based on the merits of My Son, based on His righteousness.

Come with shouting and dancing, for blessed is the one whose transgressions are forgiven, whose sins I will not count against him.

Rejoice! For **your** sins have been **forgiven**!

"…my heart stands in awe of Your words…
I rejoice at Your word like one who finds great spoil…
I hold back my feet from every evil way in order to keep Your
word. I do not turn aside from Your rules, for You have taught
me. How sweet are Your words to my taste, sweeter than honey
to my mouth!" Ps. 119:161b, 162, 101-103

Dear one, do you love My word as the psalmist did? Is it a great treasure to you, with riches just waiting for you to discover…nuggets of truth and precious gems of My faithful promises waiting for you to unearth? Is it sweet as honey to your taste so that you long for more and more choice morsels?

I tell you, feast upon My word, for it is nourishment for your spirit, and food for your soul…life for your bones. And the riches that await you there will strengthen and sustain you.

"Great peace have those who love Your law; nothing can make
them stumble." Ps. 119:165

Hope of Heaven

"By faith Abraham obeyed when he was called to go out to a place that he was to receive as an inheritance. And he went out, not knowing where he was going. By faith he went to live in the land of promise, as in a foreign land, living in tents with Isaac and Jacob, heirs with him of the same promise. For he was looking forward to the city that has foundations, whose designer and builder is God…These all died in faith, not having received the things promised, but having seen them and greeted them from afar, and having acknowledged that they were strangers and exiles on the earth. For people who speak thus make it clear that they are seeking a homeland….as it is, they desire a better country, that is, a heavenly one. Therefore God is not ashamed to be called their God, for he has prepared for them a city." Heb. 11:8-10, 13-16

My beloved, are you living in a greater, truer reality? Does the hope of heaven fill your heart? Does a longing for your real homeland burn within your soul?

You have worked so hard to make your house a home for your children…but I would remind you this morning of a different home that I am preparing <u>for you</u>.

In your labor of love and in your daily striving and toil, don't forget to look up. Don't allow the mundane tasks of everyday to obscure your view of heaven and deaden the hope that dwells within you. Look to the sky, for your redemption surely draweth nigh.

"For the eyes of the Lord move to and fro throughout the earth that He may strongly support those whose heart is completely His." II Chron. 16:9a

*I*s your heart *completely* Mine? I will not compete with another for your affections, My child.

Draw near to Me and cast away your idols from before you. Cast away the comforts you worship, the things you give your heart and emotions over to, the things you run to for peace and comfort, the things with which you try to satisfy yourself, the things you long for and feverishly pursue because you are convinced that if you can just obtain them you will have joy.

My child, these are all false supports that you have chosen to prop you up, but they are all rotted throughout and will, in the end, cave in the more you lean upon them. They cannot satisfy you and will only leave you wanting.

Leave them behind, for they are a distraction from the glorious purpose for which I have called you.

I am the *Rock* on which you can stand firm, and on which you *must* stand. Look to nothing else to fulfill or satisfy you, but to Me alone, and I will fill you until you overflow!

"For the Lord will not forsake His people; He will not abandon His heritage;
If the Lord had not been my help, my soul would soon have lived in the land of silence.
When I thought, 'My foot slips,' Your steadfast love, O Lord, held me up.
When the cares of my heart are many, Your consolations cheer my soul." Ps. 94:14,17-19

Dear child, in this time of trouble, draw near to Me and I will draw near to you. He who comes to Me I will in no way cast out. I want you to know Me more intimately, more deeply.

For I am your source of help and hope for every situation. Lay upon Me the burdens that you bear, that I may carry them for you, and your heart be light once more.

Place those whom you love into My loving hands, knowing that I will care for them as tenderly and faithfully as I care for you. Trust Me to work in their lives as I am in yours.

"The voice spoke to [Peter] again, 'Do not consider anything unclean that God has declared clean.'" Acts 10:15

My child, are you calling yourself unclean when I have declared you pure, righteous, not guilty, forgiven?

Low-grade guilt steals your joy.

Speak truth to your heart this morning… by My blood you are bought fully, cleansed completely, and loved dearly. This must be the unshakable foundation of your faith. Your acceptance before Me will not—cannot—be altered now or for all eternity by your performance, or lack thereof.

Rejoice in this truth…embrace it and cling tightly to it…keep it always before your eyes. My joy will fill your heart as you dwell on this fact…I have declared you **clean!**

"Do not forget this one thing, dear friends: with the Lord a day is like a thousand years, and a thousand years are like a day. The Lord is not slow in keeping His promise [regarding His return], as some understand slowness. He is patient with you, not wanting <u>anyone</u> to perish, but <u>everyone</u> to come to repentance." II Pet. 3:8-9
"Therefore, go into <u>all</u> the world, and preach the gospel to <u>every</u> creature." Mark 16:15

O My child, can you hear My heart in these verses, the heart of your Savior? I beseech you, implore you. It is beyond a command; it is My heart for those who are lost…My heart that <u>none</u> should perish, <u>not even one</u>…not your mother or your brother, not your neighbor, mailman, or your boss…not the woman at the grocery checkout or the person sitting next to you on the train…no one.

Hear My heart in these verses, because My heart is for them…<u>each</u> and <u>every one</u> of them. And My desire is to use <u>you</u> to bring hope to the hopeless, to unlock their captive hearts and set them free to new life in Christ.

O child, repent of your negligence, and pray that I would give you <u>My</u> heart for those who are perishing all around you. Then pray, pray, pray for them…and watch for the timely opportunities for the Gospel that I bring. Be faithful to seize each one, for each opportunity is a precious soul whom I died to rescue.

And My Spirit will go before you and loosen the hard ground, and the anointing of My Spirit will be upon you. And you will plant in good, prepared soil. And the seed will take firm root. And you will in the end reap a mighty harvest of precious souls for My glory.

"And they heard the sound of the Lord God walking in the garden in the cool of the day, and the man and his wife hid themselves from the presence of the Lord God among the trees of the garden.
Then the Lord God called to the man, and said to him, 'Where are you?'" Gen. 3:8

My child, where are you this morning?

Are you hiding from Me, avoiding My presence? Is your heart distant, have your affections for Me waned? Have you, perhaps gradually and subtly, lost your first love?

I say these things not to condemn you, My child, but to woo you back to Me. My call to you this morning is redemptive, and filled with promise, hope, joy, and grace…

Return, My beloved, return to Me.

"Awake, O sleeper, and arise from the dead, and Christ will shine on you!" Eph. 5:14

"Remember these things, O Jacob, and Israel, for you are My servant; I have formed you, you are My servant, O Israel, you will not be forgotten by Me. I have wiped out your transgressions like a thick cloud, and your sins like a heavy mist.
Return to Me for I have redeemed you. Shout for joy O heavens, for the Lord has done it!" Isa. 44:21-23a

My child,

You see your sins, but do you see My cross casting its shadow upon them?

You see all your failures, but do you see how My precious blood covers them?

You see yourself shrouded with dirty garments; I see you wrapped in robes of righteousness.

You see the black stain of your iniquities; I see you whiter than snow.

Return to Me, for I have redeemed you! Shout for joy, My child, for I have done it!

Like an ox pulling a load that is much too heavy for him to manage, I see you, My child, struggling under burdens that are much too heavy for you to bear.

You pull with all your might, you struggle and strain, but you can't budge it. You cry out to others to help and assist you, but they are helpless to move it as well. Discouragement is stripping your joy and robbing your peace.

Yet, all the while, I stand by waiting for you to humbly surrender and ask for **My** help. For you have yet to truly lay this down at My feet and let Me take it. The One who formed the worlds with the breath of My mouth and can move mountains with a word of My lips can move your mountainous burden. I am the burden-lifter, and you are yoked with Me.

You can't, I can…so let Me

"Serve wholeheartedly, as if you were serving the Lord, not men, because you know that the Lord will reward everyone for whatever good he does…" Eph. 6:7-8

My child, I call you this morning to pour out your life in wholehearted service to Me. Hold nothing back. But rather, offer up the members of your body, joyfully putting your hand to the plow and serving others in My Name…joyfully building My kingdom and investing your life and your energies in things that will last.

Busily be about your Father's business, for the time is short. Strengthen the weak, help the helpless, preach the Gospel to the lost…serve one another, for in doing so you are serving Me and are building up treasures immeasurable in heaven.

May your heart echo Paul's words to the Corinthian church, "I will very gladly spend for you everything I have, and be spent myself, for your souls." II Cor. 12:15

"For He is like a refiner's fire and like fuller's soap. He will sit as a refiner and purifier of silver, and He will purify the sons of Levi and refine them like gold and silver, and they will bring offerings in righteousness to the Lord.
Then the offering of Judah and Jerusalem will be pleasing to the Lord..." Mal. 3:2b-4

What area of your heart are you holding back and keeping from Me? You may have given over all other areas of your life, and for that I commend you. But I want **that one**...I want to help you tear down that idol you've erected and secretly bowed before day after day. I want that idol of materialism, of worldliness, of lust that you've been hiding and nurturing. And I love you enough to go after it. I love you enough to stir the pot and disturb your comfort zone in order to cause the trapped and hidden impurities to rise to the surface, that I might skim them away, leaving behind only the purest silver, which will truly reflect My glory.

"Why do you say, O Jacob, and assert, O Israel, 'My way is hidden from the Lord, and the justice due me escapes the notice of my God?'" Isa. 39:27

I knew you before the world began, and I called you by your name. I've seen each and every triumph of your life and have rejoiced with you. I've seen each and every tragedy and heartbreak of your life, and I have wept with you. Your way is not hidden from Me—not your past, not your present, and not the days to come. I see them all.

And just as I have been with you in the past, both rejoicing with you and comforting you, so I will be your constant support in the days you have yet to live.

Your way is not, and never will be, hidden from Me, My child. I am right by your side, and there I'll ever stay.

"Turn away from evil and do good; so shall you dwell forever. For the Lord loves justice; He will not forsake His saints." Ps. 37:27-28

Dear one, is your head hung in shame this morning?

Have you, as the prodigal son, 'come to your senses,' but you have made such a mess of your life that you doubt if I would even have you…if I would even take you back?

My child, hear My words this morning…even in your wanderings, I was there. I will never let you go, and there is nowhere you can hide from My Spirit.

And, even when you are running from My grace, I will search for you until I find you. I will run to you while you are still some distance away on the road and embrace you with open arms and wrap you in the robe of My righteousness.

Upon your finger I will place the ring of promise, the ring of My covenant…and I will restore you. Yes, I will make all things new.

And the latter days will be sweeter than the former, for you will walk with Me hand in hand, and I will lead you and guide you in the good way.

Let these words breathe life and renewed hope into your heart.

"But He said to me, 'My grace is sufficient for you (it is enough for you), for My power is made perfect in weakness.' Therefore I will boast all the more gladly of my weaknesses, so that the power of Christ may rest upon me…For when I am weak, then am I strong." II Cor. 12:9-10

My child, before you lies a daunting task, a calling that only you can fulfill, a work that I have called you uniquely to perform for the glory of My Name.

But this morning your heart cries out to Me, "It is too high a mountain to climb, too great a thing…and I am so small, so weak, so inadequate."

And My child, so you are! But glory in your weakness as you step out by faith in My strength, knowing that the accomplishment of things that are unachievable by man bring the greatest glory to My Name. What man declares, "Impossible!" I declare, Be done!

And, in My wisdom, I choose the small, the weak, the inadequate to accomplish My wondrous deeds, for I would not share My glory with man.

Therefore…small, frail, and weak as you are…rise up to the challenge I place before you this day and embrace it by faith—not faith in your own ability, but faith in My ability to accomplish the impossible through you! Step out in the strength which I supply, the strength of the Almighty God, and behold the wonders I will perform through a humble vessel yielded to Me!

"What is impossible with men is possible with God!" Luke 18:27

D o you <u>know</u> that I <u>delight</u> in you? I sacrificed <u>so</u> much, I <u>crushed</u> My precious Son, so that I could have a relationship with <u>you</u>, so that you could come into My presence and remain here, so that you could come and abide here in My love.

My child, how it hurts My heart, having given <u>so</u> much, when you don't come to Me…either because of the busyness of life, or because you run to other things to try to fill and satisfy your heart instead, or because you are afraid to come because of a guilty conscience.

I have <u>so much </u>here for you… overflowing fountains of blessings; mighty rushing rivers of refreshing, sweet streams of cool water to quench your thirsty soul.

Lift your head, My child, and look into the eyes of your loving Father, and see there My full acceptance and delight in you because of the sacrifice of My Son. Then come and abide here in My presence and immerse yourself in the waters of refreshing.

Picture in your mind a child running down the steps on Christmas morning, full of wonder and excitement. There is a beautiful gift under the tree with his name on it. He slowly unwraps the present to reveal an amazing kingly robe, fringed with gold and made of the finest materials money can buy. But then the child puts the lid back on the box, content to stay in his old tattered garments.

I have given you a gift, My child…a precious, priceless gift…a gift that cost Me everything. Beautiful robes of righteousness to replace the filthy rags of sin and condemnation you are wearing. But you put the lid back on the box and have never put it on…still dressed in your rags of death while a royal robe of righteousness, bought with the very life of My precious Son, remains unopened and unworn before you.

Take My gift this morning. Exchange your rags for My righteousness, receive My forgiveness, and let Me dress you in My glorious salvation this morning!

"If anyone abides in Me and I in him, he will bear much fruit; but apart from Me you can do nothing." John 15:5

Are you weary this morning? Do you feel you lack the strength to continue on the path I've laid before you? Do you feel that your efforts in My Name are ineffective and unfruitful?

I cry to you this morning, Come! I am ever waiting for you here…waiting to wrap My arms around you and embrace you once more. Yes, return to Me, abide in Me…My presence is not a place to visit infrequently…Don't be content with that! For My presence is a place where I'm calling you to stay, a place where I'm calling you to live!

Come now, and I will heal you. Come, and I will restore you. Come, and not only will I set you free, but I will use you to loose the bonds of others, and the fruit of your harvest will increase and be overflowing.

As you abide in Me, My Spirit will well up within you, refreshing and bringing renewed rest and life to your soul, and from there flowing forth to bring new life to others.

"Whoever believes in Me, out of his heart will flow <u>rivers</u> of <u>living water.</u>" John 7:38

"Awake, O sleeper, and arise from the dead, and Christ will shine on you." Eph. 5:14

Awake, My beloved…Rise up and shake off your slumber! For you have been lulled to sleep by the dark melody of the pleasures of this world and of its many comforts.

Awake, I say! For the work is great which I call you to accomplish in My Name, but the laborers are few.

I have indeed promised you rest…but it is the rest of spirit which you find as you dwell in My presence…not rest from the work to which I've called you.

Rise up! For the days are short and your life is but a breath. Put your hand to the plow in the strength and grace that I give you, and pour out your life as a living offering to Me for the glory of My Name and for the furtherance of My glorious gospel.

"For all who are led by the Spirit of God are sons of God. For you did not receive the spirit of slavery to fall back into fear, but you have received the Spirit of adoption as sons, by whom we cry, 'Abba Father!' The Spirit himself bears witness with our spirit that we are children of God." Rom. 8:14-16

Before it left your lips, I heard the cry of your heart.

Before the foundations of this world were set in place, I already had a plan for rescuing you and making you My own.

When you were naked and poor, empty and alone, I drew you to Myself and said, **Child, you are Mine.** And this morning I would once again say these sweet words, **Child, you are Mine.**

I took the rags that you wore, and placed My robe of righteousness around you. I gave you the bread of life to satisfy your aching hunger. I gave you My living water to satisfy your thirst.

Then I adopted you and brought you into My family as My own, so that you would be with Me forever…never again to be alone, never again to be in want.

Oh Yes, dear child, you are Mine.

Rejoice this morning, for I have called you **son**…I have called you **daughter**…I have called you **Mine!**

Steady Me

"If the Lord delights in a man's way, He makes his steps firm; though he stumble, he shall not be hurled headlong, for the Lord upholds him with His hand." Ps. 37:23-24

I believe the Lord gave me a picture of a little child just learning to ride a bike, and losing his balance. But, his father is behind him, firmly holding the seat, ready to grab hold of him, and saying reassuringly, 'It's okay, sweetheart. I'm here, I've got you, and I won't let go.'

Some of you this morning feel like that child...maybe you have stumbled or lost your balance as you hit some unexpected bumps on the road you are traveling. Perhaps you are fearful that you will be hurled headlong.

But I believe your heavenly Father would say to you this morning, *Dear one, it's okay. I'm here, I've got you, and I won't let go! If you begin to fall, trust in Me...for Mine is the hand that will steady you, and My grip is strong and sure.*

*"**When** you pass through the waters, I will be with you, And through the rivers, they will not overflow you. **When** you walk through the fire, you will not be scorched, nor will the flame burn you.*
For I am the Lord your God, your Savior." Isa. 43:2 (NAS)

M y child, you *will* have trials…not *if* but **when**. But know that I will bring you safely through each and every one.

So, let the storms rage all around, for I am with you:

And I will keep him in perfect peace whose mind is stayed on Me.

And let the strong winds blow fiercely…you will not be shaken:

For I will keep him in perfect peace whose mind is stayed on Me.

Though the enemy assail you, and you're reeling from the blows, though you fear your heart may fail you as you face your frightening foes…remember:

I will keep him in **perfect peace** whose mind is stayed on Me.

"The Lord will guide you continually, and satisfy your soul in drought, and strengthen your bones; you shall be like a watered garden, and like a spring of water, whose waters do not fail."
Isa. 58:11

Child, I haven't brought you this far to leave you now. Just as I led the children of Israel into the wilderness, so I have guided you to the difficult place in which you now find yourself.

But do not be dismayed! For just as I provided miraculously for My people in that desert, so I have given you, and will continue to provide for you, everything you need for life and godliness.

When there is no water in sight, I will miraculously pour out water from the rock to satisfy your soul in drought. And just as I provided the manna and quail when they had no food, I will be your sustenance and will strengthen your bones.

And though you see great barrenness around you, you shall be like a watered garden, and like a spring of water, whose waters do not fail. For I am your source and supply.

"The heavens declare the glory of God, and the sky above proclaims His handiwork." Ps. 19:1
"When I look at Your heavens, the work of Your fingers, the moon and the stars, which You have set in place, what is man that You are mindful of him, and the son of man that You care for him?" Ps. 8:3-4

Dear child, I am the God of all the universe…the Maker of all created things. I spoke whole worlds into existence with simply a word from My mouth.

Can I not affect in you the change that you so desire? Am I able to form galaxies, yet unable to touch the human heart and shape it for My glory?

You say, 'But I've tried to get victory over this area in my heart before, yet I failed.' Come again, My child, yet this time with the strength that I will supply.

You see the situation as hopeless and impossible. But with God, all things are possible!

Will you come this morning? Will you bring this thing with you…this thing that is an affront to My holiness…this stumbling block in your life that has been limiting your growth in Me? Will you bring it to the altar this morning and, with all the power of the Almighty God as your aid, we will mortify this together, once and for all?

And from its ashes will grow a sweet-smelling garden; and what was your disgrace and reproach will become a testament to My glory, My grace, and My life-changing power!

"Where shall I go from Your Spirit? Or where shall I run from Your presence? If I ascend to heaven, You are there! If I make my bed in sheol, You are there! If I take the wings of the morning and dwell in the uttermost parts of the sea, even there Your hand will lead me, and Your right hand will hold me." Ps. 139:7-10

O child, be not dismayed…for I will never leave you. There is no place you can go that My eyes are not upon you, and that My heart is not toward you. Why do you struggle so to believe this truth…to really, truly believe it?

Stop running from what alone can satisfy. Turn to Me now and find, not condemnation, but grace and My opened arms waiting to embrace you.

Come and meet Me at the cross of your salvation, and there leave all your guilt and shame. Yes, come to the cross and satisfy yourself with the sweetness of My grace…receive it…savor it…Let it flow over you and through your very being to bring new life to your spirit and strength to your bones.

"The Lord said, 'I have chosen you and have not rejected you.'" Isa. 41:9

"Hope deferred makes the heart sick." Prov. 13:12

My child, have you been broken and crushed, wounded and scarred.

Have despair, disillusionment, and weariness set in, and has hope been driven out of your heart? Your head is bowed in defeat, not in prayer, for in your heart you have said, "Can I even trust God?"

Dear one, lift your head and look into the eyes of the One who is always watching over you. You feel forsaken, but you are not. I promised you that I am an *ever present* help in your times of trouble.

Shake off the heavy chains of despair that are holding you down under their weight, seeking to make you ineffective—*shake them off!*

Rise up! Muster your faith! *Cling* to My promises yet again, for they are *yes* and *amen*, and I am *faithful* to My word! You can trust me!

Hope in Me, My child, for I am strong, and mighty to save *you!*

"[W]hen evening had come, [Jesus] said to them, 'Let us go across to the other side.' And leaving the crowd, they took Him with them in the boat. And a great windstorm arose, and the waves were breaking into the boat, so that the boat was already filling.

But Jesus was in the stern, asleep on the cushion. And they woke Him and said to Him, 'Teacher, do You not even care that we are perishing?!' And He awoke and rebuked the wind and said to the sea, 'Peace! Be still!' And the wind ceased, and there was a great calm.

And He said to them, 'Why are you so afraid? Do you still have no faith?' Mark 4:35-40

Are you, as the disciples, finding the waters of your life stirred into a great storm? Yet, instead of trusting Me, and trusting in My unfailing love for you, you charge Me as they did, saying, 'Lord, do You not even care that I am perishing?!'

I would say to you that I care much more than you know. I care enough to **allow** the storm in order to reveal the weakness of your faith; I care enough to **allow** the storm in order to show you once again the power of My might, that you might praise and glorify My Name, and that your weak faith may be strengthened.

Will you trust in Me and My love and care for you even in the midst of the tempest? Will you praise Me in the storm? And will you praise Me for the storm, knowing that I have allowed it for your good?

From Strength to Strength

"Blessed are those whose strength is in You, O Lord, in whose hearts are engraven the highways which lead to Zion.
As they go through the barren Valley of Baca ('weeping') they make it a place of springs; the early rain also covers it with pools.
They go from strength to strength." Ps. 84:5-7 (NAS)

There are some this morning who are going through this ''Valley of Weeping,' this dry and barren wasteland which seems unable to sustain any life, so desolate, so purposeless.

But, My child, My word to you this morning is… **walk on**…walk on, yet not in your own strength or you will perish. Walk on in My strength, and as you go you will watch in amazement as I transform the very landscape of this place before you. It will become a place of springs, covered with pools of life-giving, refreshing water. You will go from strength to strength.

And, My child, you will indeed go 'through' the valley, for I will surely bring you safely to the other side in My time.

And you will reach back and grab the hands of those who come behind you, others who find themselves in this desolate place. And I will use you to guide them, that from your journey you may teach others to sing songs of praise in the darkest of nights, that they too might 'walk on' and go from strength to strength.

"I am He who will sustain you. I have made you and I will carry you; I will sustain you and rescue you." Isa. 46:4 (NAS)

"He will not let your foot be moved; He who keeps you will neither slumber nor sleep. The Lord is your keeper."
Ps. 121:3-5

Have clouds of worry, doubt, fear, and unbelief rolled in and cast shadows on your soul?

This morning I tell you, do not look at your circumstances and be swallowed up by them, sinking into despair.

Instead, I call you this morning to 'come up higher' on the wings of My Spirit. Lift your eyes and keep your gaze fixed upon Me, and you will see then that behind the clouds the sun still shines, and I am ever faithful to My promises, and they remain true and sure. I am the One who keeps you. Take heart…have hope. Look with the eyes of faith.

"I lift up my eyes to the hills. From where does my help come? My help comes from the Lord, the maker of heaven and earth." Ps. 121:1-2
"So let us <u>know,</u> let us press on to <u>know</u> the Lord. His going forth is as certain as the dawn; and <u>He will come to us</u> like the rain, like the spring rain watering the earth." Hos. 6:3 (NAS)

My child, to <u>you</u> I call this morning…<u>know Me</u>…know Me as your loving Father; know Me as your faithful Friend, the Friend that sticks closer than any brother; know Me as your Savior, as the One who died in your place to set you free from sin and give you life everlasting.

I cry to you this morning, <u>Come</u>! Don't search for another to fill your need or the empty longing of your heart. For in Me, and Me alone, will you find all that you seek, all that you need. I will fill you up to overflowing. I will truly be your all-in-all.

Yes, I call to you this morning…<u>Come</u> and <u>know</u> Me. Come <u>just as you are</u>. Bring your sin-sick, weary soul to the foot of the cross and let Me wash you there until you are whiter than snow.

You say, "My sins are <u>many</u>." But to <u>you</u> I say, My blood covers a <u>multitude</u> of sins. Yes, though your sins are many, I will wash them in My blood which I shed <u>for you</u>…and they will be no more.

<u>Come</u> and <u>know Me</u> this morning, and you will know peace…and you will find joy.

"How precious is your steadfast love, O God! The children of mankind take refuge in the shadow of your wings. They feast on the abundance of Your house, and You give them drink from the river of Your delights." Ps. 36:7-8

My beloved, come…and feast upon Me. Come and partake at My table of delights. Come and be filled to the fullest measure with the goodness of your Lord, and let your soul be satisfied with My kindness and grace…for they are sweeter than honey and are poured out lavishly upon you in a constant flow.

Be attentive to all that I have set before you today. See that not a crumb goes to waste. Partake yourself, and then offer these choice morsels to others, that they, too, can be fed and nourished, strengthened and sustained.

Bring them, bring them all,…compel them to come…for there is room at My table for all who hunger, and abundant supply which never dwindles. And all who come will be satisfied.

"Ask, and it shall be given to you; seek, and you shall find; knock, and it shall be opened to you…for everyone who asks receives, and he who seeks finds, and to him who knocks it shall be opened." Matt. 7:7-8 (NAS)

My child, what is it that you lack this morning? I am here and am able to abundantly provide. What is your pressing need? Ask according to My will, and you can have full assurance and confidence that I will do it!

Is not this whole world and all it contains in the palm of My hand? Am I not the Creator and Sustainer of all you see? Come and ask this morning… come full of faith in My power…come full of faith in My love and care for you.

Above all, know that I am here…I am with you.

I will never leave you on your own. We'll trod this path together. Each challenge or difficulty is just another opportunity for you to lean on Me, and another opportunity for Me to show you what a faithful, loving God you serve!

"They will be called oaks of righteousness, a planting of the Lord for the display of His splendor." Isa. 61:3b

My child, picture yourself looking down at a tiny seed that you are holding in your hand.

My child, you are looking at yourself and your life like that little seed and saying, 'There is nothing here of value, nothing God can use. My life is small and insignificant.'

But *I* know all that I have planted within you. I know what you will become as you live your life in the sunshine of My presence, as I water you with My Spirit, as you receive the rich nourishment from My word.

You may not look like much right now in your own eyes, and maybe even in the eyes of others. But in *My* eyes, I who see the end from the beginning…, I see the mighty oak which has yet to emerge from the small seed. I see the oak of righteousness that will display My splendor.

I challenge you this morning to see your life through My eyes, eyes filled with vision and faith for what you will become through Me.

"Blessed is the man who trusts in the Lord and has made the Lord his hope and confidence.
He is like a tree planted along a riverbank, which sends out its roots by the stream, and its roots reach deep into the water. He does not fear when the heat comes, for his leaves remain green, and he is not anxious in the year of drought, for he does not cease to bear fruit." Jer. 17:7-8 (NAS)

My child, do you believe that I have the best for you?

Have I failed you *ever*, that you should doubt Me now? Remember my faithfulness to you in sending My Son, born as a babe. Remember My faithfulness to you at the cross. Remember My faithfulness to you over the years of your life.

When the strong winds blow, and difficulties arise, do you find yourself bending low and swaying to-and-fro at their mercy, threatening to topple if the storm rages on against you? Do you find yourself anxious in the year of drought; when hard times come, do your leaves begin to wither, your fruit begin to lessen or fail?

I say again, blessed is the man who trusts in the Lord and has made the Lord his hope and *confidence*! Send down your roots deep, and draw of the waters of My stream. And when the pressures of life come, you will not be shaken, you will not be moved. You will be able to stand firm, strong and steadfast. And even in time of heat and drought, you will not fear nor be anxious, for your leaves will remain green, and you will not cease to bear fruit.

"Why are you in despair, O my soul? And why have you become disturbed within me? Hope in God, for I shall again praise Him for the help of His presence, the Lifter of my countenance and my God.
O my God, my soul is in despair and downcast within me; Therefore, I remember You..." Ps. 42:5-6a (NAS)

Yes, My dear child, *remember Me.* Do not think that your circumstances are careening out of My control and that your life is hidden from My watchful eye. No, My child...I see...*I see...*

Yes, *remember Me*. And though your soul is in despair, remember that I am a safe harbor, a shelter from the storm that assails you, and run to Me. And though you are suffering greatly, remember that I am the God of great comfort. Find refuge in the shadow of My wings, and peace in the warm embrace of My presence. Though you feel shaken and pressed on every side, know that I am *for* you, not against you.

In the midst of your pain, *remember Me* and come receive the help of My presence and the comfort that only I can give...the comfort of your loving Father, who sees, and who cares more deeply than you know.

"You make known to me the path of life; in Your presence is fullness of joy; at Your right hand are pleasures forevermore."
Ps. 16:11

My child, I love you with an everlasting love. Come warm yourself by the fire of My presence. Let the icy frost of indifference melt away from around your heart.

Stay here with Me until the radiating warmth of My love has permeated every part of your being and you are once again utterly and wholly Mine…until once again your heart burns with passion for Me and for the things of God…until you are once again filled with vision and hope instead of despondency and despair…until once again joy is set ablaze within you.

Come, gather at the fire…

"Hear my prayer, O Lord! And let my cry for help come to Thee. Do not hide Thy face from me in the day of my distress; Incline Thine ear to me; In the day when I call answer me quickly." Ps. 102:1-2 (NAS)

I hear your cry, My child...I hear your cry.

And not from a distance have I heard the groanings of your heart, for I am with you, by your side.

When you have wept, I have wept, too...for you are My precious child whom I love and it breaks My heart to see your heart broken.

Come now...grief and sorrow have washed over your heart like waves. Let Me wash over your heart with My comfort and wrap My strong arms of love around you and hold you near. Come now...let My peace and sweet presence be like a balm to bind up and heal your aching heart, My beloved.

"Why do you say, O Jacob, and speak, O Israel, 'My way is hidden from the Lord, and my cause is disregarded by my God'? Have you not known? Have you not heard? The Lord is the everlasting God, the Creator of the ends of the earth. He does not faint or grow weary; His understanding is unsearchable. He gives strength to the weary, and He increases the power of the weak. Even youths grow tired and weary, and young men shall stumble and fall exhausted; but they who hope in the Lord shall renew their strength; they shall mount up with wings like eagles; they shall run and not be weary; they shall walk and not faint." Isa. 40:27-31 (NAS)

"The Lord is near to the brokenhearted and saves the crushed in spirit." Ps. 34:18

"A [tender] bruised reed He will not break." Is. 42:3

But rather...

"He heals the brokenhearted and binds up their wounds." Ps. 147:3

My child, I speak tenderly to you this morning...I am near. Do not think that your circumstances, shattered dreams, and disappointments have evaded My watchful eye. Bring your wounded heart to the foot of the cross; for I am a man of sorrows and acquainted with grief, and I am not unable to sympathize with you in your pain. But rather, in Me you will find sweet comfort like no other can offer. And I will heal you and restore you...And I will turn your sorrow into joy.

Do not allow your face to remain downcast, but rather 'look up'! For, behold, I am doing a new thing! Have abundant faith and vision for your future, as I have...for I am already there, and I see the beautiful, wonderful things I have in store that will be wrought in your life. Truly, the best is still before you!

241

"For I know the plans I have for you, declares the Lord, plans for welfare (good) and not for evil, to give you a future and a hope!" Jer. 29:11

Yes…I will once again fill your heart with hope!

Therefore, "Sing to the Lord a new song; sing His praise from the end of the earth!" Isa. 42:10a

"Christo in you...the <u>hope</u> of <u>glory!</u>" Col. 1:27b

Jesus, for the <u>joy set before</u> Him, endured the cross. Are you, for the joy set before you, enduring with perseverance and grace the trials in your own life? Does the hope of glory...the hope of heaven...brighten everything you do, and lighten every step you take?

Look up! You <u>must</u> keep your eyes fixed on things above; for I, the Almighty God, the Creator of the heavens and the earth, still reign upon My throne! The God of endless mercy still reaches down His hand of forgiveness and grace to <u>you</u> this morning, to draw you nearer still.

Take hope in this glorious fact...I have gone to prepare a place for you, that where I am you may be also. So let your spirit rejoice and your heart be filled with joy this morning, for you will be with Me forever in the place I have prepared <u>for you</u>! <u>Hope</u> in this!

"In Thy book they were all written, the days that were ordained for me when as yet there was not one of them." Ps. 139:16b (NAS)

From your youth, I have carried and sustained you. All these years, through trials and storms, through victories and triumphs, can you look back and see that My hand was in yours?

Even before you knew Me, I knew you by name. Even through your darkest times, I was with you.

In light of this, look forward with bright hope and trust for your future in Me, not fearing what it may bring, but knowing that I will be with you…holding you by the hand, protecting you, leading and guiding you in the way you should go, faithfully watching over you and guarding you in all your ways.

I have been walking with you all this time, all these years. I will *certainly continue* to shower your life with My love, faithfulness, and care for the rest of your days. Rejoice and hope in this truth…in this promise!

O My child, you are precious to Me. I have made you just the way you are, and you are so special to Me.

You may look around you at other people and say, "I'm not good at <u>anything</u>!" But I would say to you, I have a special job for you to do for Me that you were uniquely gifted for. Yes, I have given you gifts and talents, and as you draw closer to Me, I will reveal to you what they are.

I have created you for a purpose…My purpose. Live your life for Me and Me alone…an audience of One. No one else's opinion is really important if you are living your life according to My plan for you, putting one foot in front of the other, and stepping out in the direction in which I lead you…one step at a time.

"But Zion said, 'The Lord has forsaken me; my Lord has forgotten me.'
Can a woman forget her nursing child, that she should have no compassion on the son of her womb?
Even these may forget, yet I will not forget you. Behold, I have engraved you on the palms of My hands..." Isa. 49:14-16a

My child, I love you with an *everlasting* love...never doubt that. While it was out of love for, and obedience to, the Father that I went to and suffered the cross...it was also out of My love for you, My chosen one. I endured the cross because of the joy set before Me not only of being united again with Him, but also of sharing the rest of forever—all eternity—with *you.*

Truly I say to you again, I have *loved* you, and *not* forsaken you. I have chosen, desired, and loved...*you!*

"When the poor and needy seek water, and there is none, and their tongue is parched with thirst, I the Lord will answer them; I the God of Israel will not forsake them. I will open rivers on the bare heights, and fountains in the midst of valleys. I will make the wilderness a pool of water, and the dry land springs of water…that they may see and know, may consider and understand together, that the hand of the Lord has done this, the Holy One of Israel has created it." Isa. 41:17-20

Do you come poor and needy this morning, parched with a thirst that you can find no water to quench?

Call to Me and I will answer you and not forsake you. And I will satisfy you with Myself, for I am the Living Water. Drink of Me, and you will never again know thirst.

Do you come with empty hands this morning…nothing to offer, nothing of yourself to give? I will fill your empty hands of My abundance and will satisfy your soul with My goodness. And you will no longer be in want but will be overflowing from a heart that is filled up with Me. Lift your hands to Me now and receive.

And you will have more than enough to sustain yourself, and will overflow in good measure to others who hunger and thirst, that they too may be filled.

Eyes On The Prize

"Do you not know that in a race all the runners compete, but only one receives the prize? Run in such a way that you may obtain it!" I Cor. 9:24

My child, are you still **running** this race, or have you slowed your pace and become lax? Perhaps the pursuit of comfort has drawn your attention and gaze away from the prize, the great reward for which you are competing, and you've lost the vision.

Or perhaps you are weary, and discouragement and despair have whispered to you the lie that this is a race which you can't possibly win…you're not strong enough…you're not good enough…you just don't have what it takes.

But I would say, I am the One who called you not only to run this race, but to win it. Give Me your all, press on and persevere with all that is within you, and you will find then that My strength will carry you when your strength fails.

You have but one life to live, one race to run.

Set your eyes on the prize and run with all your might in the strength which I supply. And you will finish even stronger than you started!

"Like a shepherd He will tend His flock, in His arms He will gather the lambs, and carry them in His bosom; He will gently lead those with their young." Isa. 40:11

I believe there are some moms this morning whose hearts are racked with pain and whose cheeks are stained with tears, either because of the way you perceive your children are turning out, or because you find yourself in a situation where you are raising them alone…your spouse being either physically or emotionally absent.

I would say to you this morning, My beloved one,

I *Am*…

I *Am* their heavenly Father, even before you were their mother, for I knew them by name even before they were conceived in your womb and had already numbered all of their days.

I *Am* your Husband who will never leave or forsake you. I am an ever-present help in your times of trouble, and I will guide you and give you wisdom.

I *Am* the Rock that you can, and *must*, lean upon when you are weary, when you see no fruit from your labors, and when fear for the future threatens to swallow you up…lean on *this* rock, lean on Me; I will give you the strength to do that which I've called you to do…to be a godly mother to your children and a Christ-like example for them to follow.

I *Am* carrying you, My love. Rest in My arms and trust in My goodness and My heart…for you and for your children.

Hope in Me and look brightly on the future, not with fear or dread, for I will never let you go or leave *you* alone, *OR* your *children*! In My love I will pursue them just as I have pursued you and won your heart, My child. *I Am*… and I am *enough!!*

"And when he came to the gate of the city, behold, a widow was there gathering sticks. And he called to her and said, 'Bring me a little water in a vessel, that I may drink.' And as she was going to bring it, he called to her and said, 'Bring me a morsel of bread in your hand.' And she said, 'As the Lord your God lives, I have nothing baked, only a handful of flour in a jar and a little oil in a jug. And now I am gathering a couple of sticks that I may go in and prepare it for myself and my son, that we may eat it and die.' And Elijah said to her, 'Do not fear; go and do as you have said. But first make me a little cake of it and bring it to me, and afterward make something for yourself and your son. For thus says the Lord the God of Israel, "'The jar of flour shall not be spent, and the jug of oil shall not be empty, until the day that the Lord sends rain upon the earth.'" And she went and did as Elijah said. And she and he and her household ate for many days. The jar of flour was not spent, neither did the jug of oil become empty, according to the word of the Lord that he spoke by Elijah." I Kings 17:10-16

My child, miracles happen when the impossible is surrendered to Me and laid on My altar. As long as you are still trying to accomplish a thing in your own strength and with your own wisdom, I cannot work. It is when you step aside, realizing that you are unable, incompetent, lacking in power of wisdom, and you lay it humbly before Me, asking for My help and having full assurance of faith in My power to accomplish what you cannot; that is when you will see the mighty hand of God move on your behalf.

Have confidence in Me…place all your trust in Me…for what is impossible with man is possible with God!

"Trust in the Lord with all your heart, and lean not on your own understanding. In all your ways acknowledge Him and He will make straight your paths." Prov. 3:5-6

"I am the resurrection and the life. Whoever believes in Me, though he die yet shall he live." John 11:25

When I rose that first Easter morning, I brought new life to all who would believe on Me, I brought new hope to those whose hopes had been shattered, and I brought new joy to those who mourned and were troubled.

Today I ask you…will you let Me rise in *your* heart? Believe in Me and let me breathe new life into you this morning. Let Me cause new hope to rise in your heart and replace *your* shattered dreams…new hope that will never disappoint.

Let Me infuse your spirit with new joy…joy that is not dependent on your circumstances…joy that springs forth as a fountain and that no one can take away from you.

Come to the empty tomb this morning and see…for I am risen *indeed*…and I desire to be risen in *your* life *today*, for *today* is the day of salvation!

"For this very reason, make every effort to supplement your faith with virtue, and virtue with knowledge, and knowledge with self-control, and self-control with steadfastness, and steadfastness with godliness, and godliness with brotherly affection, and brotherly affection with love. For if these qualities are yours and are increasing, they keep you from being ineffective or unfruitful in the knowledge of our Lord Jesus Christ. For whoever lacks these qualities is so nearsighted that he is blind, having forgotten that he was cleansed from his former sins." II Pet. 1:5-9

My child, through the cross you are forgiven—it is finished. But are you daily being sanctified, being changed?

It is only as you come and receive of My love that you can give it out. You **want** to be changed, to exhibit the fruits of My Spirit, but this can only happen as you linger in My presence, beholding My face, receiving of Me.

As you rest in the peace of My presence, I will do the surgery needed to remove those besetting sins of your heart and instead replace them with all that is Me: love, joy, peace, forgiveness, putting others' needs and interests before your own, patience, kindness, goodness, faithfulness, gentleness, self-control…

You cannot rush the Surgeon as He does His delicate work, cutting away with His scalpel what should not be, and bringing healing and rightness.

Transformation happens here in My presence. Do not leave until you are changed.

You deserve to be called **'rejected,' 'cast away,'**…but I call you **'My friend.'**

You deserve to be called **'deserted,' 'forsaken,'**…but I have adopted you into My family.

You deserve to be called **'condemned,' 'guilty,'** and to have the full fury of My wrath poured out upon you…yet instead I have declared you **'forgiven'** and called you **'My son,' 'My daughter.'**

I draw you now into My presence by My grace. Let your heart take great comfort in this…not by your merits do I bid you come and commune with Me, but by My grace which I have freely and lavishly poured out upon you.

This is My never-changing, never-ending grace, which has changed the verdict over your life once and for all, eternally binding and secure forever, shouting its joyful declaration down through the halls of eternity, *This one is Mine!… Pure… Holy… Righteous… **Forgiven!***

"Change me, God," you cry! But you run into My presence, list your requests of Me, then run back out. You do not linger; you do not wait; you do not rest and abide.

You will be changed as you *tarry* in My presence and allow Me to do My work in your heart. You will be changed from glory to glory…that is, as you enter into My glorious presence and remain long enough for Me to touch your heart. The more you linger here, the more you will want to remain here.

Your heart will be set aright, not when you are satisfied to give Me a passing glance, but when your eyes are *set* on Me.

"'Yet even now,' declares the Lord, 'return to Me with all your heart, with fasting, with weeping, and with mourning; and rend your hearts and not your garments.'
Return to the Lord your God, for He is gracious and merciful, slow to anger, and abounding in steadfast love." Joel 2:12-13

O h child,

There is a storm that rages within your heart this morning. And I am the only One who can still the troubled waters of your soul.

Return to Me this morning, I say to you, My child. You may feel like you have fallen too far. But you are only ever a whispered prayer away from My arms, only ever a heart's cry away from My loving embrace.

Return to Me, My child, and you will find, not condemnation, but rather restoration. Yes…I will restore you.

If you hear these words this morning, do not harden your heart. For it truly is you that I call. I came not for the well, but for the sick. Return to Me this morning and let Me heal you.

"For the Lord your God is gracious and merciful and will not turn away His face from you, if you return to Him." II Chron. 30:9b

Grace, grace I speak to you this morning!

Your heart cries out, "How did I get to this place? How have I fallen so far?"

But to you I would say, Is *My arm so short that it cannot save?*

You can never fall so far that My hand cannot reach you.

You can never fall so far that when you turn I won't be right there, waiting to forgive, waiting to restore.

"All your sons will be taught of the Lord; and the well-being of your sons will be great." Isa. 54:13 (NAS)

I see your tears for your children, this morning.

I see your anxiousness over some of the things they have done, and the perceived state of their hearts.

You *fear* for your children, but I call you to *pray* and have *faith* for them. Their sin shocks you so; yet you forget how foolish your heart was and all of the dark places which I brought *you* out of in *your* journey with Me over the years.

And, just as I have been faithful, steadfast, and trustworthy in *your life,* so will I be for your children. I am at work in their lives just as I have been in yours, although you cannot see it with your earthly eyes.

Hold onto My promises for your children. For My plans for them are good, and My love for them is great.

Commit them to Me, trust Me with them, and know that they are in My capable hands and I hold them with a sure grip.

"Christ in you, the hope of glory." Col. 1:27

My child, I love you so much! Love is a word vastly overused, but My love for you far exceeds any you have ever known, for it is unconditional and everlasting. Nothing, and no one, can change, alter, or diminish the perfect love that fills My heart for you.

My love for you is eternal—I loved you before the world began, and I knew you by name before I even created you in your mother's womb.

My love is limitless and ever-flowing toward you. It will never end…ever!

And I have gone before you to prepare a place for you, that you will one day soon be with Me always. I am anxiously waiting for you on the other side, My heart yearning to be with you face to face, anticipating our joyous reunion, and looking forward to showing you around this spectacular place which I have prepared for you and to sharing in your delight and wonder and awe at all that I have created to bless you!

Does your heart yearn for Me as Mine does for you, My love? Does anticipation of seeing Me face to face make your heart beat faster as Mine does? Does the hope of glory, the hope of heaven, swell your heart with renewed courage and strength to carry on?

Look heavenward to the One who loves and waits for you!

"Therefore, brothers, since we have confidence to enter the holy places by the blood of Jesus, ...and since we have a great Priest over the house of God, let us draw near with a true heart in full assurance of faith, with our hearts sprinkled clean from a guilty conscience...Let us hold fast the confession of our hope without wavering, for He who promised is faithful." Heb. 10:19-23

Have you forgotten My Gospel of grace, My child? Have you forgotten that you were cleansed from your sins by the blood of My son? Are you listening to your guilty conscience as it seeks to condemn you this morning, or are you holding fast the confession of your hope without wavering?

I bid you, come this morning...

Come into the holiness of My presence with confidence by the blood of Jesus, which covers you. Draw near to Me in full assurance of faith and with conscience cleansed. Do not waver in the confession of the hope that is within you, instead hold fast...for I who promised am faithful.

"Why are you in despair, O my soul? And why have you become disturbed within me? Hope in God, for I shall yet praise Him, the help of my countenance, (my salvation) and my God." Ps. 42:11 (NAS)

Do not despair, My beloved child. For from the cross of your salvation radiates a *glorious hope.* For you are in My hand and I will not let you go – I will keep you. The future is bright before you, and your inheritance is sure. There stands a place in heaven prepared for *you.*

Let this hope rise in your heart; embrace it, live in the good of it, and let that hope give birth to great joy!

"I waited patiently for the Lord; He inclined to me and heard my cry. He drew me up from the pit of destruction, out of the miry bog, And set my feet upon a rock, making my steps sure."
Ps. 40:1-2

There are some this morning that find themselves caught in a quagmire of sin and despair, much like the character Christian in the book Pilgrim's Progress. And the more you struggle and try in your own strength to free yourself, the deeper you seem to sink.

But I call you to look up, this morning…for My arm of grace is extended and I am an ever-present help in time of need. Place your hand trustingly in Mine and let Me do for you what you could not do for yourself. Let Me lift you up out of the miry clay and free you from the pit which has engulfed you and sought to swallow you up.

Then I will set your feet firmly on the rock. And I will put a new song in your mouth, a song of praise for My glorious grace and deliverance. And many will see, and put their trust in Me.

"If we are faithless, He will remain faithful; for He cannot deny Himself." II Tim. 2:13

Dear one, My love for you does not change when you are negligent of Me. Though it saddens My heart greatly when you don't fellowship with Me, I love you none the less.

I will always remain faithful to you, because that is *who I am*. And you will always remain My dearly beloved child, for that is *who you are* to Me!

Your self-sufficiency and willful independence grieve Me, but they make you no less **Mine!**

For My love for you is not about you…whether or not you behave as you should or do the things you ought. My love for you is all about *Me*…My father's heart to love even the wayward, unruly, prodigal child and bring him back home—not because he is worthy in and of himself, but because *he is My son* and I *love* him!

Child, you are Mine, and I will love you forever and always. Will you come home to Me this morning?

"We are afflicted in every way, but not crushed; perplexed, but not driven to despair; persecuted, but not forsaken; struck down, but not destroyed...
So we do not lose heart...For this light and momentary affliction is preparing for us an eternal weight of glory beyond all comparison, as we look not to the things that are seen but to the things that are unseen. For the things that are seen are transient, but the things that are unseen are eternal." II Cor. 4:8-9, 16-18

There are those this morning who strongly identify with Paul in this passage. You, too, feel afflicted in every way, perplexed, persecuted, and struck down.

Yet, Paul was able to view his trials and sufferings as light and momentary...How?...Because the hope of heaven filled his heart.

Does the light of heaven fill your eyes this morning, and are you blinded to all else by the glory of it as Paul was? Then you will begin to see your trials and afflictions in light of eternity, and as light and momentary.

Therefore, do not lose heart. Walk on in courage and strength with your face set toward heaven. And remember… You are not home yet.

The Joy of the Cross

"Speak tenderly to Jerusalem, and cry to her that her warfare is ended, that her iniquity is pardoned, that she has received from the Lord's hand double for all her sins." Is. 40:2

I have not repaid you as your sins deserve, but rather I have lavished My grace upon you and abundantly pardoned your iniquities!

Rejoice this morning, My people, for your sins are no longer counted against you! Shout for joy to the Lord your God, for I have opened your eyes and revealed to you My sweet and wonderful salvation!

"Oh sing to the Lord a new song, for He has done marvelous things! His right hand and His holy arm have worked salvation for Him. The Lord has made known His salvation; He has revealed His righteousness in the sight of the nations. He has remembered His steadfast love and faithfulness to the house of Israel. All the ends of the earth have seen the salvation of our God. Make a joyful noise to the Lord, all the earth; break forth into joyous song and sing praises!" Ps. 98:1-4

"For we do not have a high priest who is unable to sympathize with our weaknesses, but one who in every respect has been tempted as we are, yet without sin. Let us then with confidence draw near to the throne of grace, that we may receive mercy and find grace to help in time of need." Heb. 4:15-16

I speak comfort to you this morning, My people…for I am the God of all comfort.

And even though you feel weak and helpless, I call you to look to the throne of grace this morning, for there stands your risen Savior full of power and might, and able to save!

So, look to the throne of grace even now, and there find hope…hope to stay the course…hope for My almighty power and strength to aid you in your weakness…hope that, just beyond the realm of what can be seen, is Someone infinitely greater than your circumstances, Someone who loves you without measure, and who desires to come to your aid even more than your heart yearns to be helped.

"'In an outburst of anger I hid My face from you for a moment; but with everlasting lovingkindness I will have compassion on you,' says the Lord your Redeemer.
'For this is like the days of Noah to Me, when I swore that the waters of Noah should not flood the earth again. So I have sworn that I will not be angry with you, nor will I rebuke you. For the mountains may be removed and the hills may shake, but My lovingkindness will not be removed from you, and My covenant of peace will not be shaken,' says the Lord who has compassion on you." Isa. 54:8-10 (NAS)

My child, My *covenant* to you is an *everlasting* covenant…forever written in heaven…one that will *never* be *broken*.

My covenant to you is *steadfast* and *unchanging*. My covenant of peace with you *will not be shaken!*

For it is a covenant written in My blood on the cross; it is a covenant signed and sealed by My sacrifice for you.

I have declared for all eternity…

You are Mine!

"Therefore I tell you, do not be anxious about your life, what you will eat or what you will drink, nor about your body, what you will put on…Look at the birds of the air; they neither sow nor reap nor gather into barns, and yet your heavenly Father feeds them. Are you not of more value than they? And which of you by being anxious can add a single hour to his span of life? And why are you anxious about clothing? Consider the lilies of the field, how they grow; they neither toil nor spin, yet I tell you, even Solomon in all his glory was not arrayed like one of these. But if God so clothes the grass of the field, which today is alive and tomorrow is thrown into the oven, will He not much more clothe you, O you of little faith? Therefore do not be anxious, saying, 'What shall we eat?' or 'What shall we drink?' or 'What shall we wear?' For the Gentiles seek after all these things, and your heavenly Father knows that you need them all. But seek first the kingdom of God and His righteousness, and all these things will be added to you. Therefore do not be anxious about tomorrow…" Matt. 6:25-34a

Precious child,

Do not fear for the future, for I am with you, and I love you, and I care about everything that is going on in your life. Not one minute detail escapes Me. Not one need is unknown to Me.

So trust Me, child…I <u>will</u> supply. I will give you all that you need for life and godliness in abundance as you seek Me above all else. If I provided for your greatest need upon the cross when I rescued you from the penalty of your sin by taking it upon Myself, will I not provide for you everything else that you need?

Trust Me, My child…

"Oh, taste and see that the Lord is good! Blessed is the man who takes refuge in Him!" Ps. 34:8

My child, how sweet is My presence to the one who enters…how warm My embrace which awaits him. How tender each choice word I speak to his heart, for they bring strength, encouragement, life, and peace.

To you I would say this morning, draw near and be embraced. Drink deeply of My lovingkindness. Partake of each precious morsel I speak to your heart.

Come and be refreshed!

Taste and see that I am good!

"Moreover, Josiah put away the mediums and the necromancers and the household gods and the idols and all the abominations that were seen in the land of Judah and in Jerusalem that he might establish the words of the law of the Lord...
Before him there was no king like him, who turned to the Lord with all his heart and with all his soul and with all his might...nor did any like him arise after him." II Kings 23:24-25

D o you love what I love? I am calling you to make a sober assessment of your heart—What do you dwell on in your thoughts? What do you talk about? What do you desire more of, even lust after and crave?

Just as Josiah tore down the idols in the land, I call you to ruthlessly tear down the idols that you have erected in your heart—each and every one—until nothing remains there but Me. Yes, place Me above all else. It is only when you tear these idols down and set your affections on Me that you will be truly satisfied.

"'Return to Me and I will return to you,' says the Lord of Hosts." Mal. 3:7

My little lamb, do not cower away from me; for I come not to crush, but to restore you. I bring in My hand not a scepter of judgment, but a staff with which to lead you home.

See…I have left the 99, and have sought you out this morning in your wandering. I tenderly call to you as you tremble there, bleeding in the briars, in the entrapments of your own sin and ungodly choices…sins that I have covered by My grace.

But you say, 'I'm not even sure of the way back, and I feel too weak to even attempt to make the journey.'

But I say to you, I will lift you up out of the thorns, I will put you on My shoulders, and I will carry you…for I know the way. And though you are weak, I am strong.

And though you were faithless, I remain faithful. Fall upon the everlasting arms of your Good Shepherd, and let Me bring you home this morning.

There are some this morning who are experiencing the stripping away of everything you depend on, and your heart is very anxious. Picture with Me a man stepping from a bright, sunny day into a dark cloud where he can't even see his own hand in front of him. I would encourage you not to be anxious, but to trust Me. I would encourage you with these words from **Jeremiah 31:**

vs. 9

With weeping they shall come, and with pleas for mercy I will lead them back; I will make them walk by brooks of water, in a straight path in which they shall not stumble...

vs. 16

Thus says the Lord: Keep your voice from weeping, and your eyes from tears, for there is reward for your work, declares the Lord...

vs. 17

...There is hope for your future.

"Therefore behold, I will allure her, bring her into the wilderness, and speak kindly to her. Then I will give her her vineyards from there, and the Valley of Achor as a door of hope. And she will sing there as in the days of her youth, as in the day when she came up from the land of Egypt." Hos. 2:14-16 (NAS)

My child, I am here with you this morning. I have **never** left you, nor will I **ever** go away from you.

Open your heart to Me now, and rejoice in the sweetness of My presence as you have in times past. Come once again to the cool, refreshing waters. You have allowed your heart to become hard—let me soften it again here in this place of closeness with Me. Let Me water the dry, cracked places of your heart where you have allowed resentfulness and bitterness to choke out the growth and life.

And once again, as you draw from My water of life, you will see new growth and beauty springing forth in the wilderness of your heart.

You will see all the barren places covered once again with luscious foliage and rich new fruit.

My presence is here with you, surrounding you even now. Open your heart wide and drink deeply of My life-giving water.

"And the seven priests carrying the seven trumpets of ram's horns before the ark of the Lord went on continually, and blew the trumpets; and the armed men went before them, and the rear guard came after the ark of the Lord, while they continued to blow the trumpets. Thus the second day they marched around the city once and returned to the camp; they did so for six days.
Then it came about on the seventh day that they rose early…and marched around the city in the same manner seven times…
And it came about at the seventh time, when the priests blew the trumpets, Joshua said to the people, 'Shout! For the Lord has given you the city!'…So the people shouted, and the priests blew the trumpets; and when the people heard the sound of the trumpet, the people shouted with a great shout and the wall fell down flat." Josh. 6:13-16, 20a (NAS)

What great walls loom before you this morning?

What formidable gates are barring your way? I tell you to praise Me! Praise Me in the face of insurmountable trials! Praise Me when you see no earthly hope for victory!

Praise Me—with all of your might praise Me! And watch as My mighty hand brings down the walls before you and levels the mighty fortress that stood in your path.

The obstacle that you thought was insurmountable you will watch crumble beneath My all-powerful hand as you praise Me.

"How precious also are Thy thoughts to me, O God! How vast is the sum of them!
If I would count them, they would outnumber the sand." Ps. 139:17-18 (NAS)

O My beloved, how tender are My affections toward you this morning. My heart swells with love for you, love deeper than you could ever fathom. What joy fills My heart when you come and receive of My love.

Don't question My love for you and shrink back. For My love for you is *sweet* and *rich* and *endless* in its supply. It is *everlasting* and *will not cease*. My faithfulness to you is *steadfast* and *never-changing*; it will continue *forever!*

Make My joy complete this morning by coming and receiving of My love, which I lavish upon you even now. Just reach out and take the hand that beckons to you…rapturous joy awaits you with arms opened wide!

Walking in the Light of Grace

Lord, please wash my guilty conscience clean. Set me free from the subtle guilt that weighs down my heart and makes me feel condemned before you. For You said that there is now **no** condemnation for those who are in Christ Jesus. And because I am in Christ Jesus, there is now therefore **no** condemnation **for me!**

Lord, You set me free from sin and death; now please help me to **live** in the **reality** of that freedom. Your Son has set me free, and I am free indeed.

I will let Your cleansing waters flow over me now, that I may fully realize and take hold of the fact that there is **no stain** upon me because of Your work on the cross.

I will choose to walk this day in the brilliant, glorious light of Your amazing grace. For I am forgiven…It is finished!...and I am received warmly by my Father in heaven.

In the blood of My Son I have washed you completely,

Upon you there is no stain;

Every part of your heart, each dark corner and crevice,

Cleansed white and made new again…

Therefore, let no guilty conscience remain!

"What man of you, having a hundred sheep, if he has lost one of them, does not leave the ninety-nine in the open country, and go after the one that is lost until he finds it? And when he has found it, he lays it on his shoulders, rejoicing. And when he comes home, he calls together his friends and his neighbors, saying to them, 'Rejoice with me, for I have found my sheep that was lost.'" Luke 15:4-6

Oh, My child…it is **you** that I came to search for and find this morning. You have wandered to a dark place, but I desire to bring you back. I am calling out your name this morning. Will you hear my voice? I beckon you to return with Me. Will you come?

Will you be found by Me?

"Take heed to the ministry which you have received in the Lord, that you may fulfill it." Col. 4:17 (NAS)

My children, I have given to each of you various gifts…gifts to be used in ministry to Me, gifts to be used in ministering to My people, gifts to be used to reach a lost world with the hope of salvation.

There is one body, yet many different parts, each with a unique function, and that which every joint supplies is vital to the working of the whole.

I would ask this morning, is there any lack in the body that exists because you are not fulfilling the ministry to which I have called you? Is there a weakness in any area because you are not using your God-given ministry, gifting, or talent? Are you holding back, waiting to see if another will step in and accomplish the task?—But I have called you!

Are you gifted in hospitality? Then ask how you may use it to further My kingdom. Are you gifted as an evangelist? Then look for the opportunities I send your way and seize each one. Do you have the gift of prophecy? Then regularly ask Me what I desire to speak to My people.

This is not a stern word, but rather a gentle reminder, that those gifts were given to you <u>by Me</u> and <u>for My glory</u>, and to further My kingdom. Be faithful with what you have been given, and I will bless you with even more!

"He who dwells in the shelter of the Most High, will abide in the shadow of the Almighty. I will say to the Lord, 'My refuge and my fortress, my God, in whom I trust!'…
He will cover you with His pinions, And under His wings you may seek refuge; His faithfulness is a shield and bulwark… You will not be afraid of the terror by night, Or of the arrow that flies by day;… For you have made the Lord, my refuge, Even the Most High, your dwelling place." Ps. 91:1-9 (NAS)

My child, come and be refreshed in My presence, that you may be able to stand strong against the assaults of the enemy as he seeks to blow you to and fro this day.

Your fortitude and strength are replenished and shored up in your quiet times with Me, as you come and dwell in the secret place, the shelter, of the Most High God.

And you will not fear the wiles of the enemy, nor will you bow under his attacks. For you will be hidden beneath the shadow of My wings, and you will rest within the mighty fortress that is your God. And I will be a shield about you, a mighty bulwark and a great wall on your every side. And I will hem you in before and behind. And you will not be afraid, but rather will look on and see as My mighty hand moves on your behalf. For I am the One who will deliver you.

"Knew ye not that I must be about My Father's business?"
Luke 2:49 (Web.)

W hat thing have **I** called you to? Put your hand to the plow and don't look back! What thing have **I** placed on your heart? Run to the task!

Don't look for and wait around for others to step up. I've called **you**. Don't intellectualize, don't rationalize, don't look for all the reasons why you can't do it, or why you won't be successful in the matter.

For what I've **called** you to, I will **equip** you to do. And to that which **I've** called you, I will in abundance provide all that you need and will pour out gifts upon you to succeed in the task.

Take the first step, and watch My grace unfold before you. Take the first step—place your foot into the waters that lie before you—and watch Me part them. And as you step out in My will, you will walk out onto dry ground. And I will be with you every step of the journey.

"'For I know the plans I have for you,' says the Lord. 'They are plans for good and not for disaster, to give you a future and a hope.'" Jer. 29:11 (NLT)

My child, I have plans *for you* this very day— plans for you to walk in to accomplish My purposes *this day*. Look for the opportunities I bring you today—the people I bring across your path to minister to need renewed hope and vision; those to whom I would have you speak a word of encouragement to lift their spirits and to lift their eyes back to their Savior; those dying of thirst in the desert of this world who need the Living Water you can give them—who need a Savior; those who are sick and who need someone to just take initiative, be obedient, and lay hands on them and pray for them to be healed.

Oh, I have much work to do, much I desire to accomplish just in this next twenty-four hours. Will you step up and walk in the plans I have for *you* this day?

Come once again into the sweetness of My presence and be *energized* for the tasks ahead. Here in My presence is fullness of joy—*this* is where your *strength* comes from. *Here* you'll find *all you lack*. Then go and accomplish My purposes for this day, knowing that the time is short!

"The Spirit of the Lord God is upon Me, because the Lord has anointed Me to bring good news to the afflicted, He has sent Me to bind up the broken-hearted, to proclaim liberty to captives, and freedom to those who are bound; to proclaim the favorable year of the Lord, and the day of vengeance of our God; to comfort all who mourn, to grant all of those who mourn in Zion, giving them a garland instead of ashes, the oil of gladness instead of mourning, the mantle of praise instead of a spirit of fainting." Isa. 61:1-3a (NAS)

My child, why are you downcast? You look at the upheaval and chaos that the world is in, and your heart despairs. You see the darkness getting darker, and your heart sinks and faints within you.

But did I not tell you it would be so? And have I not prepared you for just such a time as this? Have I not chosen you to reveal My salvation in this hour? To preach good news to those who are afflicted, to bind up the wounds of those who are broken-hearted, to set those free who are bound up in the chains of sin, to comfort those who are mourning, to shine forth My light so brilliantly against the backdrop of the blackness of this world that people will see My glory and meet their Savior?

Do not be downcast, but rejoice and shine forth My light!

"As they were gathering in Galilee, Jesus said to them, 'The Son of Man is about to be delivered into the hands of men, and they will kill Him, and He will be raised on the third day.'"
Matt. 17:22-23

Just as I promised My disciples, I *was* raised up on the third day.

What have I promised you that as of yet remains unfulfilled? Maybe the salvation of a loved one, maybe a burden for some type of ministry that I've birthed in you, maybe a promise of provision. Let hope rise again in your heart. For what I have told you, that will I do. Don't mourn and weep for it as if it were dead forever. For I will raise up that thing which I have spoken to you in secret. And it will be raised in glory and power—the life-giving, hope-giving, resurrection power of God!

Instead of allowing doubt to envelop you, let hope rise anew this morning in your heart, just as the sunrise on that third day that found My tomb empty and My wondrous promise fulfilled.

Hope and believe, and you will see My glory!

"You make known to me the path of life; in Your presence there is fullness of joy." Ps. 16:11

Do you lack joy this morning? Have I not told you that you will find it in My presence? But instead of engaging your heart, instead of coming into My life-giving presence to receive joy and strength, you act as one unforgiven, shrinking back, standing in the doorway of My outer courts, looking on from a distance, but not drawing near to Me.

Press through, My child, My redeemed one…press through by the blood which covers you and cries 'worthy'! For I have redeemed you and called you 'My child'…You are Mine!

Climb the steps to My throne. Rest here in the presence of the One who loves you, and your joy will be full.

"But Zion said, 'The Lord has forsaken me; my Lord has forgotten me.' Can a woman forget her nursing child, that she should have no compassion on the son of her womb? Even these may forget, yet I will not forget you." Isa. 49:14

My child, I have loved you with an everlasting love. Surely I have not forgotten you. Look! I have engraved you on the palms of My hands, and your name I bear on My heart. Child, you are Mine.

And though you see in yourself nothing loveable, I see the one for whom I died. Though you see in yourself the loathsome, the detestable, the unworthy, I see the blood of My Son which covers you and makes you whiter than the newly fallen snow, and I see My dear child whom I bought and redeemed and adopted as My own!

Yes, I rejoice over you with great joy, My child.

In you is My delight. As a father delights in his children, so do I greatly delight in you. Listen as I speak your name with tender affection.

This morning draw near, knowing that I have not forsaken nor forgotten you, knowing that you are fully accepted because of the blood of My Son, and let Me show you My great love and delight in you!

"For God so loved the world, that He gave His one and only Son, that whoever believes in Him should not perish, but have eternal life." John 3:16 (NIV)

My child, I loved **you that much**!! All that I suffered, all that I endured— to save you…yes! But also so that I could have a relationship with you!

And now, My child, there is a world outside these doors that I love, people outside these walls that I died to save and that I long to enjoy a relationship with as well. They are dying; they are lost; they are utterly hopeless; they need to be rescued… they need **Me**.

Will you be My feet and go to them in My Name? Will you be My hands and touch them? Will you be My arms and embrace and love them? Will you be My mouth to introduce them to your best Friend and tell them of a Savior who made a way where there was no way to save them from the hell their sins deserve? Will you tell them of One who loves them so much that He died in their place so that He could spend **eternity with them?**

"But now listen, O Jacob, My servant; And Israel, whom I have chosen: Thus says the Lord who made you and formed you from the womb, who will help you, Do not fear,...For I will pour out water on the thirsty land and streams on the dry ground; I will pour out My Spirit on your offspring, And My blessing on your descendants; And they will spring up among the grass like poplars by streams of water. This one will say, 'I am the Lord's,'...and that one...will write on his hand, 'Belonging to the Lord.'" Isa. 44:1-5 (NAS)

There are some this morning who are anxious about where they perceive their children's hearts to be right now and are concerned about their salvation and their walk with God. But I want to reassure you with these words:

Do not fear, My child. Rather, trust Me; for I will draw *them* to Myself just as I drew *you*. And another generation will see My faithfulness and will rise up and praise Me.

In the day-to-day, be faithful to point them to the Savior; in the mundane help them to see the hand of God moving on their behalf. Do not be anxious for them, but pray in faith, believing that I am for them, *not against* them, and that I *love* them and *desire* to draw them to Myself. I have a plan for their lives, a wonderful plan; and though you can't see it right now, know that I am working out My plan to perfection even now. Trust Me, and trust in My heart of love for your children. I will do it.

"…God loves a person who gives cheerfully. And God will generously provide all you need. Then you will always have everything you need and plenty left over to share with others. …For God is the One who provides seed for the farmer and then bread to eat. In the same way, He will provide and increase your resources and then produce a great harvest of generosity in you. Yes, you will be enriched in every way so that you can always be generous. And when we take your gifts to those who need them, they will thank God." II Cor. 9:7-8, 10-12 (NLT)

I have loved you with an everlasting love…child, you are Mine. And because I love you, and because you are My child, will I not care for you as you give to My work?

Truly I say to you, trust Me…step out, have faith and believe. Trust in the promises of My word…the very promises I made to you.

For where there is lack, I will pour out of My abundance; and where there is need, I will fill up to overflowing—for I am a faithful God and a compassionate, caring and providing Father.

Yes, I will be your abundant provision in all things as you step out to build My kingdom. Sow the seed I've supplied you with liberally. Freely you have received—trust Me now, and freely give!

"Who is a God like You, who pardons iniquity and passes over the rebellious act of the remnant of His possession? He does not retain His anger forever, because He delights in unchanging love. He will again have compassion on us; He will tread our iniquities under foot. Yes, Thou wilt cast all their sins into the depths of the sea. Thou wilt give truth to Jacob and unchanging love to Abraham." Mic. 7:18-20 (NAS)

My child, in whom is all My delight, come and dance before Me in fields of splendor this morning, for I have **pardoned all** your sins! Worship Me with a loud shout and a song of joy for My fathomless and unchanging love toward you! Lift up your hands before Me at the foot of the cross, where your burdens were lifted and your death penalty removed!

Yes, rejoice this morning, for I have had compassion on **you!**

Your sins are gone Cast to the depths of the sea I've ransomed and redeemed you Set you completely free!

"O sing to the Lord a new song, For He has done wonderful things, His right hand and His holy arm have gained victory for Him. The Lord has made known His salvation; He has revealed His righteousness in the sight of the nations." Ps. 98:1-2 (NAS)

O My child, truly I have done marvelous things. Not only did I ransom and redeem you, not only did I make you My own and call you 'My child', not only did My blood cover all your sins and wash you clean, but I went one step farther—I imputed the righteousness of My Son to you—I clothed <u>you</u> with <u>His</u> glorious righteousness, righteousness that shines brighter than the noonday sun!

I would say to you this morning, let your light so shine among men that they may glorify your Father who is in heaven.

"Arise, shine; for your light has come, and the glory of the Lord has risen upon you…For behold, darkness will cover the earth, and deep darkness the peoples;
But the Lord will rise upon you, and His glory will appear upon you. And nations will come to your light, and kings to the brightness of your rising!" Isa. 60:1-3

"These things I have spoken to you, that in Me you may have peace. In the world you have tribulation, but take courage; I have overcome the world." John 16:33 (NAS)

My child, why do you despair? Why do you lose heart? For I am still on the throne, and I reign with strength and power over all things—the turmoil in the world, and the turmoil in your own life and circumstances.

Don't look at the waves that seek to engulf you; look to the One who has all power to still them. If you are beginning to sink, grab My outstretched hand, and I will lift you up above the stormy sea. Yes, I will place you firmly on the rock and make your footing sure.

Do not despair; do not lose heart.

Rather, look to the One who can save you, and hope!

There are those this morning who believe that their sins outweigh My boundless grace and inexhaustible forgiveness. You may have never said it, but in your heart there is guilt and condemnation over past sins that is trying to strangle your life in Christ. I want to encourage you this morning with the words of Isaiah 57:18-19:

""I have seen his ways, but I will heal him; I will lead him and restore comfort to him and to his mourners, creating the praise of their lips.
Peace, peace to him who is far and to him who is near,' says the Lord, 'and I will heal him.'" (NAS)

"The afflicted and needy are seeking water, but there is none, and their tongue is parched with thirst." Isa. 41:17a (NAS)

My child, does this verse describe you this morning? Afflicted, needy, seeking but not finding, tongue parched with thirst?

But My child, listen to the rest of this passage.

Hear My promises to you:

"I, the Lord, will answer them Myself, As the God of Israel I will not forsake them. I will open rivers on the bare heights, and springs in the midst of the valleys; I will make the wilderness a pool of water, and the dry land fountains of water." (NAS)

Yes, My child, you thirst...but I will pour out upon you of Myself...and not sparingly will I give, but I will pour out in abundance and will satisfy your thirst with My Spirit overflowing! So come to the waters and drink deeply...come and be satisfied in Me!

"Surely our griefs He Himself bore, and our sorrows He carried; Yet we ourselves esteemed Him stricken, Smitten of God, and afflicted. But He was pierced through for our transgressions, He was crushed for our iniquities; The chastening for our well-being fell upon Him, and by His scourging we are healed." Isa. 53:4-5 (NAS)

My child, don't forget all that I accomplished on the cross that day <u>for you</u>…

I bore <u>your</u> griefs, and I carried your sorrows; I was pierced through for your sins,

I was crushed for <u>your</u> wrongdoings; The punishment for <u>your</u> peace fell upon Me,

And by My scourging you are healed.

Don't forget, My child…don't forget!

"Now it came about when his master heard the words of his wife, which she spoke to him, saying, 'This is what your slave did to me,' that his anger burned. So Joseph's master took him and put him into the jail, the place where the king's prisoners were confined; and he was there in the jail.
But the Lord was with Joseph and extended kindness to him, and gave him favor in the sight of the chief jailer. And the chief jailer committed to Joseph's charge all the prisoners who were in the jail so that whatever was done there, he was responsible for it. The chief jailer did not supervise anything under Joseph's charge because the Lord was with him; and whatever he did the Lord made to prosper." Gen. 39:19-23 (NAS 1977)

A re you aware of the kindness of the Lord in the midst of your trial?

I have not left you alone in the battle. For truly I am with you—your strong tower, your faithful aide and constant companion.

Are you aware that throughout your difficult circumstances I have sustained you, enabled you to endure by providing strength and encouragement, sent you provision and help in time of need, ministered to your spirit.

Look for My goodness and kindness in the midst of the storm.

"being confident of this very thing, that He who has begun a good work in you will complete it until the day of Jesus Christ;"
Phil. 1:6 (NKJV)

My child, I have begun a deep and wonderful work in your heart. Do not fear that this work will be short-lived and waning, that the embers of the fire I've ignited in your heart will grow dim and fade away. I will complete the work I began.

Come into My presence daily and let Me water your spirit and refresh you. Let Me fan into flame what I started. Yes, press into Me and feast on My word, for it will renew your mind.

And remember, child, it's not so much your grip on **Me**, but rather My firm, strong, never-failing grip on **you!**

I will keep you…

I will **never** let you go!

"If any of you lacks wisdom, let him ask God, who gives generously to all without reproach [disapproval], and it will be given him. But let him ask in faith, with no doubting." Jas. 1:5-6a

There are some this morning who are facing decisions and they are desperate for wisdom to know what My will is in their circumstances.

I would say to you this morning:

Do you believe in your heart that I am a good Father to My children? Would a good father allow his child to wander into danger or allow the child he loves to stumble off a steep precipice because he would not show him the safe and right way to go?

So, My child, I will not allow you, as you seek wisdom from Me, to walk the dangerous path outside of My will.

My child, seek wisdom in the abundant counsel of godly men and women, for I can speak My will through these. Devour My word, which gives rich wisdom and renews your mind.

And seek the face of your *faithful, good* heavenly Father to lead you and guide you in the straight path of My will, knowing that it is My *heart's desire* to do this for you, My beloved. Do not doubt, but stand *firm* and *confident* in faith that I *will answer!*

"How blessed is the man who does not walk in the counsel of the wicked, nor stand in the path of sinners, nor sit in the seat of scoffers! But his delight is in the law of the Lord, and in His law he meditates day and night. And he will be like a tree firmly planted by streams of water, which yields its fruit in its season, and its leaf does not wither; and in whatever he does, he prospers." Ps. 1:1-3 (NAS)

My child, are you eating of My word as I have asked you to? My word is My love letter to you— read it, meditate on it, savor it; let it reassure your heart before Me this morning.

Let its words renew your mind. Drive down your roots into the good, rich, nourishing soil so that you may be strengthened and firmly planted and not shaken or uprooted by the storms of life.

Feast on My word as you would tasty morsels, and you will be a strong tree, firmly planted with deep roots by streams of life-giving water. And you will bear an **abundance** of fruit. And **your** leaf **will not** wither. And in whatever you do, you will prosper.

"Behold, the eye of the Lord is on those who fear Him, On those who hope for His lovingkindness, To deliver their soul from death, And to keep them alive in famine. Our soul waits for the Lord; He is our help and our shield. For our heart rejoices in Him, Because we trust in His holy name. Ps. 33:18-21 (NAS)

Walk one day at a time as I lead you and guide your steps and provide for you. Do not project to the future with a heart full of fear.

Have I not said I would be with you? Have I not said I would supply? Have I not said that **I** am your **help** and your **shield** and that I would deliver your soul from death and keep you alive in famine?

I will give you your **daily** bread. Each morning, awake with renewed faith and hope in your heart that I will provide just as I faithfully did the day before.

John 14:27b says, ""Do not let your heart be troubled, nor let it be fearful.'" (NAS)

There are some this morning who are struggling with fear. But I would say to you:

Peace—peace I speak to you, My child. Do not be troubled of heart. Do not anxiously and fearfully look around you. For you are not alone. The Almighty God, the Creator of the ends of the earth—I stand beside you. I have <u>never </u>left you, and I <u>never</u> will. I, even I, am the Warrior that will <u>battle</u> for you…your shield and your defense.

<u>Hope</u> in Me. Is My arm so short that it cannot save? Or am I so weak that I cannot rescue and deliver you? No, My child.

<u>Hope</u> in Me. For strength will rise within you as you place your hope in Me and wait upon Me.

"Do not be afraid any longer, only believe!" Mark 5:36 (NAS)

"Peace I leave with you; My peace I give to you; not as the world gives, do I give to you." John (NAS)

My children, do not be anxious this morning and let the enemy of your souls rob you of the peace I have blessed you with.

Kingdoms rise and fall; leaders rise and fall...but is it not My hand that places each one in their seat of power for My purposes? And whoever it is that sits on their earthly throne, do I not still reign sovereignly and with all power and authority from Mine?

Pray and trust, My children. Pray for a righteous, godly leader. Yet trust that if that does not happen it is not because I am weak or have not heard your cries. It is that My hand has placed in power the man or woman of My choosing for a purpose that you cannot see or understand right now.

Pray and trust, and let My peace reign in your hearts and minds.

"The steps of a man are <u>established </u>by the Lord, when He delights in his way." Ps. 37:23

Are you aware this morning, My child, that your times are in My hands? I have numbered all your days. Your steps are being ordered and established by Me. I know when you lay down and when you rise up. I know each word you will speak before you even utter it. I have encircled you behind and before, hemming you in on every side, and have laid My hand upon you.

In this time of shaking and uncertainty in your life, let these words from Psalm 139 bring great security to your heart and be an anchor for your soul:

"In Thy book they were <u>all written</u>, the days that were ordained for me, when as yet there was not one of them." Ps. 139:16 (NAS 1977)

Take hope, My child, and walk forth with courage; for I am establishing <u>your</u> steps, and I <u>delight </u>in your way!

"I will try to walk a blameless path, but how I need your help, Lord, especially in my own home, where I long to act as I should." Ps. 101:2 (TLB)

There are those this morning…parents, teens, and children…who would confess that this is the cry of their heart, as well.

Beloved, I would speak this truth to your heart this morning:

My child, it is true that you are not acting as you should, especially in your own home, even though I see your heart and that you desire to. You long to change, you long to walk a blameless path, but you feel powerless to do so. The more you try, the more you seem to fail.

Humble yourself and cry out to Me for help this morning, My child. Remember, you cannot do this in your own strength, for it is not by might, not by power, but by My Spirit only that this change can take place in your heart.

"I will __instruct__ you and __teach__ you in the way you should go; I will __counsel__ you with My eye upon you." Ps. 32:8

M y child, this morning you find yourself at a crossroads. There are two or more roads before you, and you are wavering with uncertainty as to which way you should go.

But hear clearly my words of instruction:

I tell you this morning that I will direct you and make it clear to you the path which leads to life, the way of My choosing, the way which is for your good and for My glory.

Will you follow Me down this road?

With reckless abandon, will you follow me?

"What happiness for those whose guilt has been forgiven! What joys when sins are covered over! What relief for those who have confessed their sins and God has cleared their record. There was a time when I wouldn't admit what a sinner I was. But my dishonesty made me miserable and filled my days with frustration. All day and night Your hand was heavy on me. My strength evaporated like water on a sunny day until I finally admitted all my sins to you and stopped trying to hide them. I said to myself, 'I will confess them to the Lord.' And you forgave me! All my guilt is gone!" Ps. 32:1-6 (TLB)

M y child, *this* is *why* I came!

"Those who hope in the LORD will renew their strength. They will soar on wings like eagles; they will run and not grow weary, they will walk and not be faint." Isa. 40:31 (NIV)

What are you hoping in right now, My child?

Are your eyes fixed upon Me, and is your heart filled with the hope of heaven and being together with Me face to face because of My finished work on the cross for you? Or have you lowered your eyes and put your hope in the things of this world, or perhaps even earthly leaders?

Things promise happiness and joy, yet they leave you empty and wanting more. Leaders promise change and hope, but they come and go, and many of their promises fade like a vanishing mist.

Lift your eyes, My child, to the One who keeps every promise and whose word stands firm and true. **Hope in Me**, and your strength will be renewed.

"Therefore, since we have been justified by faith, we have peace with God through our Lord Jesus Christ. Through Him we have also obtained access by faith into this grace in which we stand, and we rejoice in hope of the glory of God." Rom. 5:1-2

"My heart has heard you say, 'Come and talk with Me, O My people.' And my heart responded, 'Lord, I am coming.'" Ps. 27:8 (TLB)

My child, does your heart yearn as the Psalmist's did to answer My call this morning? Will you come and fellowship with Me? For My desire is for you, to commune with you, to be with you, to spend time with you. Will you enter into My presence now and let Me warm your heart in the embrace of My overflowing and abundant love for you?

"Peace I leave with you; My peace I give to you; not as the world gives, do I give to you. Let not your hearts be troubled, neither let them be afraid." John 14:27

My child, you cry out this morning for Me to lift the cloud of despair and heaviness that seems to shroud you.

My dear one, your heart is heavy and your eyes are downcast…but your eyes are the very problem!

I would call you this morning to **look up** and cast your gaze once again on the Lover of your soul, on the only One who can help, on the One who waits anxiously for your prayer of **faith** to fall on His ears.

Dear child, you have forgotten that your God is greater than any challenge you face; you have forgotten the goodness of your God and His faithfulness to you in times past; you have forgotten that your God is **for** you, not against you; you have forgotten that I will never abandon you, **especially** in your troubles; you have forgotten that I **love** you and that I am the One holding your hand.

Keep these truths always and forever before your eyes. This morning, choose to put faith over fear.

"Your Word is a lamp to my feet and a light to my path." Ps. 119:105

I desire to lead you, My child. But you need to be in My Word to receive My instructions. I desire to light your path and make the way clear to you, but you need to be in My Word.

I desire to guide you, but you must read the guidebook I've provided you. My words of light and life, guidance and instruction, purpose, provision, and hope are within these pages. Dig for them as for a treasure. Search for them as for great riches and priceless jewels. Be a people saturated by My Word. Live in it; feast upon it; love and cherish it; and let it shine the way brightly before you.

Be in My word so that you can be about My business.

"For we are His workmanship, created in Christ Jesus for good works, which God prepared beforehand, that we should walk in them." Eph. 2:10

Some of you are discouraged this morning. It seems that who you really want to be in Christ is someone you'll never become. Your failures and shortcomings loom large before you, telling you that you will never be the Christian you long to be.

My beloved child, just as a sculptor, when he looks at the block of clay he desires to fashion, does not see a block of clay but sees only the figure he wants to create and removes everything that is not part of that image, so I am chiseling away at everything in your life that is not who I am creating you to be. I am uncovering and removing, one bit at a time, the sins of your heart and whittling away with My chisel of grace at everything that is not part of the finished sculpture that I am envisioning.

And what will be revealed when I am done is something altogether glorious—it will be the face of My precious Son. See yourself through the eyes of your Father, and find great hope in what I am creating of your life!

"Beloved, we are God's children now, and what we will be has not yet appeared; but we know that when He appears we shall be like Him, because we shall see Him as he is." I John 3:2

Do you fear the next step, My child?

But wasn't I with you as you took the last? Haven't I carried you through all of life's storms up to this point? Remember all the times you trembled as you made critical life decisions in the past, only to look back later and clearly see that My loving hand was guiding you all the while in the way that I knew was best?

So be strong and courageous and take the next step which is before you without trembling or being dismayed, for I am with you wherever you go.

"And let us not lose heart in doing good, for in due time we shall reap if we do not grow weary." Gal. 6:9 (NAS)

My child, have you lost your heavenly perspective? Do you feel swallowed up by the duties and cares of the day-to-day? Maybe you're someone who has great dreams of doing mighty things for Me, but you feel trapped in a dull, and seemingly insignificant, life.

But I would say to you this morning:

I am not only the God of the great, but I am the God of the mundane, the everyday, the ordinary. I want you to make Me a part of all that you do. I desire that you would offer up to Me as a sacrifice the daily, trivial things. I want to be an integral part of everything in your life, My child. I want you to live in My presence. I want you to breathe in and out of My Holy Spirit all day long.

For no act is trivial when it is done for My glory.

Instead, it is transformed into something holy and wonderful. So do all that you do to the glory of God. Lift up before Me as a sacrifice all the things that you do, and offer them to Me in worship. And each one will be to Me a sweet fragrance; each seemingly insignificant act will be great in My eyes.

"As the mountains surround Jerusalem, so the Lord surrounds His people from this time forth and forevermore." Ps. 125:2
"Have you not known? Have you not heard? The Lord is the everlasting God, the Creator of the ends of the earth. He does not faint or grow weary; His understanding is unsearchable."
Isa. 40:28

I would remind you this morning, My child, of Whose you are. I am the Almighty, the Creator of the heavens and all they contain, the Creator of the earth and all that dwells therein. Yet, as mighty as I am, I have called you 'friend'. I have promised to surround you as My people from this time forth and forever. I do not slumber or sleep; nor do I grow weary.

No, I am intimately aware of all that concerns you. And, My child, I would remind you this morning that in your weakness (and I know you feel weak right now as you face great challenges) I am so strong. You have all the glorious power of the Almighty at your disposal. So hope in the Lord, for I will yet save you!

"He who dwells in the shelter of the Most High will abide in the shadow of the Almighty. I will say to the Lord, 'My refuge and my fortress; my God, in whom I trust!" Ps. 91:1-2

When the storms rage, dear one, I am your shelter. When troubles surround you, I am your hiding place. When the enemy assails you, I am your refuge of safety and a mighty fortress to protect you.

Where are you running for refuge right now, My child? Are you running only to well-meaning friends who can offer pity and a sympathetic ear? Or are you running to your Father, the God of the universe? My arms of refuge are here, and I am waiting to help and comfort you; waiting to protect you within the strong walls of My mighty fortress; desiring— even longing—to give you refuge from the storm that threatens to engulf you. Will you run to **Me** this morning? I am waiting for you.

"When you pass through the waters I will be with you; and through the rivers, they will not overflow you. When you walk through the fire, you will not be scorched, nor will the flame burn you.
For I am the Lord your God." Isa. 43:2-3a (NAS)

My child, you feel like you are being pummeled on every side, like you are reeling from one blow right after another.

But I would say to you, fear not, My child…for I am with you!

Are you surprised at the fiery ordeal you are going through and the troubles that assail you seemingly on every side? My child, notice My words…I didn't say if you walk through the waters or flames, but **when.**

You cry out, "My God, have you forsaken me? Where are you?" Didn't I promise you I would be with you, My child? I say to you again…I am **right here**…I am **with you!**

Look forward with the eyes of hope and faith, for I will bring you through this.

I am with you; I will guide you; I will carry you; I will sustain you; and ultimately I will give you victory and bring you **through** to the other side!

Like the sun's rays streaming through the clouds on a dark day, so is this hope which I speak to you this morning…Hold fast to this hope!

"What I want from you is your true thanks; I want you to fulfill the promises you made to Me. I want you to call upon Me and trust Me in your times of trouble, so that I can rescue you, and you can give Me glory." Ps. 50:14-15 (TLB)

My children, do not let fear rise up in your hearts. You hear of wars and rumors of wars, but do not fear. You hear the anticipation of destruction and tales of foreboding. Yet I would say to you, *Peace, be still*. I am mighty to save, and I have never forsaken those whose hearts are truly Mine. So call upon Me, My dear ones, and trust Me in your times of trouble, and watch My hand of deliverance go forth for you.

For I *will* rescue you, and you will give Me glory and honor and praise for My faithfulness and kindness to you!

"And you were dead in your trespasses and sins…But God, being rich in mercy, because of His great love with which He loved us, even when we were dead in our transgressions, made us alive together with Christ - by grace you have been saved - …" Eph. 2:1, 4-5

My mercies are new every morning, child.

Have you embraced My mercy this morning? Have you let the life-giving reality flow over you this morning that you are *completely forgiven*, that I have washed you whiter than snow and there is now no stain upon you? Have you received the truth into your spirit that you now have peace with Me and can come with confidence into My presence knowing that I fully accept you and love you?

When My Son died for you on the cross, He proclaimed "It is finished." And My child…*it is!* No more sacrifices to be made to cover your sins. It is finished—you are clean.

Embrace this mercy this morning!

"But the angel of the Lord spoke to Philip saying, 'Arise and go south to the road that descends from Jerusalem to Gaza.' (This is a desert road.)
And he arose and went; and behold, there was an Ethiopian Eunich, a court official of the Ethiopian Queen, and he had come to Jerusalem to worship. And he was returning and sitting in his chariot, and he was reading the prophet Isaiah.
And the Spirit said to Philip, 'Go up and join this chariot.' And when Philip had run up, he heard him reading from Isaiah and said, 'Do you understand what you are reading?' And he said, 'How can I understand unless someone tells me?'" Acts 8:26-31 (NAS 1977)

My child, will you go where I send you, although it makes no sense to you? Even to the desert road, will you let My Spirit lead you?

Will you preach what I tell you? For I will fill your mouth with My words if you are but a willing vessel.

Will you bring My light of hope to those who walk in darkness, and help bring sight to those who are spiritually blind?

"For whoever will call upon the Name of the Lord will be saved. But how shall they call upon Him in whom they have not believed? And how shall they believe in Him whom they have not heard of? And how shall they hear without a preacher?"
Rom. 10:13-14 (NAS)

"Therefore we do not lose heart, but though our outer man is decaying, yet our inner man is being renewed day by day. For these momentary and light afflictions are producing for us an eternal weight of glory far beyond all comparison. So we fix our eyes not on the things which are seen, but on the things that are not seen; for the things which are seen are temporal, but the things which are not seen are eternal." II Cor. 4:16-18 (NAS)

My child, your troubles seem so large before you, but that is because your view of heaven is so small. Set your eyes to look toward the *eternal*; let a vision of My glorious heaven, the place I've prepared for you to enjoy…let *that* consume your thoughts. Would you fret so, My child, if you knew that tomorrow you would be with Me? Let your troubled mind find peace and great joy as you anticipate meeting your Savior face-to-face. And then, truly, your troubles, great as they may be, will pale and truly seem light and momentary in light of eternity in glory with Me.

"I waste away; I will not live forever. Leave me alone, for my days are but a breath." Job 7:16 (NAS)

With only one life to live, My child, would you waste this day on folly? Your days are short, even as a vapor, on this earth. Would you squander even one of them?

Or would you purpose in your heart to look for where the hand of God is moving, where My Spirit is working, the things that your Father is about, and set **your** hand to those things as well?

What sense is there in putting your energies toward things that are meaningless and won't last? Don't settle for living a miniscule life, going through the motions of everyday.

Beginning today, set your eyes on My eternal purposes, and be about a heavenly mission.

Every day of your life, starting with this very day, live the adventure of walking in My Spirit.

I believe the Lord has given me a picture of Jesus hanging on the cross and a figure laying prostrate a little way off, face in the dust.

I believe the Lord would say to some today:

You have come this morning, and this is good. But you lay paralyzed by your guilt and shame. Your unworthiness looms large before your eyes.

But My child, for this I died.

The weight of your sin and your burden of guilt are keeping you down and preventing you from drawing nearer to the cross, where you would hear me say to you so lovingly…

My child, for this I died.

So now, cast off your chains of guilt this morning and the heavy burdens of your sin and unworthiness that threaten to crush you, for they are burdens meant to be laid upon My shoulders. Cast them off! Let them hold you back and keep you from the nearness of My presence *no longer*! For I have fully forgiven you…I have *completely* pardoned.

My child, for this I died.

Now freely come…you are forgiven. Draw near to Me, and let My words of mercy, grace, and love for you be as a sweet, healing balm upon your heart.

Come near to Me, for you are My beloved child, and for *this* I died!

There are those this morning who find themselves despairing... You see the current economic state of your country and how it has cast a looming shadow of enormous debt and consequences upon the future of your nation--and your children.

You see the decisions being made, some of which will affect the unborn, and others of which may affect some of the freedoms and blessings you have enjoyed up to this point.

But I would encourage your heart with these verses this morning and would *remind* you that I am in control, and you must *trust* in Me, *wait* upon Me, and *hope* in Me.

"I would have despaired unless I had believed that I would see the goodness of the Lord in the land of the living.
Wait for the Lord; Be strong, and let your heart take courage.
Yes, wait for the Lord." Ps. 27:13-14 (NAS)

"Then turning toward the woman He said to Simon, 'Do you see this woman? I entered your house; you gave Me no water for My feet, but she has wet My feet with her tears and wiped them with her hair. You gave Me no kiss, but from the time I came in she has not ceased to kiss My feet. You did not anoint My head with oil, but she has anointed My feet with ointment. Therefore I tell you, her sins, which are many, are forgiven— for she loved much." Luke 7:44-47a

D o *you* love Me much, My child? Are you willing to be broken and spilled out in devotion and love for Me as this woman was, pouring out the very essence of your life as an offering of adoration?

How *pleasing* such sacrifices are to Me! Such acts of devotion and love move the heart of your Savior, for I *delight* in extravagant devotion.

So don't hold back, not even with regard to the most costly and precious things in your life! Pour yourself out before Me, and I will fill you up with Myself, and the joy of your salvation will overflow!

"Let your eyes look straight ahead, fix your gaze directly before you. Make level paths for your feet and take only ways that are firm. Do not swerve to the right or the left; keep your foot from evil." Prov. 4:25-27 (NIV)

My child, you love Me; I see this. And although you desire to walk in the way I have for you to go, you find the path before you hazy and obscured and cannot discern the way.

But I would say to you:

Be at peace, My child, and do not fear. I will not leave you in this place but will bring you along the good path. Cast your eyes upon Me, for I am the One that will make the path level before you and show you the ways that are firm so you may place your feet on solid ground with each step. I am the only One who can lift the haze that shrouds your way and make the path clear before your eyes. Take one step at a time as I reveal it to you, and trust that, when you do, the next step will also be revealed at the proper time when you need it. Fix your gaze upon Me, and I will lead you.

"Moreover, they made an oath to the Lord with a loud voice, with shouting, with trumpets, and with horns. And all Judah rejoiced concerning the oath, for they had sworn with their whole heart and had sought Him earnestly, and He let them find Him. So the Lord gave them rest on every side…
…But the high places were not removed from Israel." II Chr. 15:14-15, 17 (NAS)

My people, have you torn down the high places in your life…those alternative altars erected to things or people who beckon you to worship them and give them first place in your heart? Have you torn them down…those things that beguile you and lure you with their charms and their fleeting pleasures, those things you love to bow before, that promise to satisfy your desires and bring you joy and fulfillment but only leave you empty and wanting, even *craving*, more of their bewitching goods?

Tear them down this morning, My children!

Worship at My altar alone.

"For the eyes of the Lord move to and fro throughout the earth that He may strongly support those whose heart is completely His." II Chr. 16:9 (NAS)

"Then Gideon said to God, 'If You will save Israel by my hand as You have said, behold, I am laying a fleece of wool on the threshing floor. If there is dew on the fleece alone, and it is dry on all the ground, then I shall know that You will save Israel by my hand, as You have said.' And it was so…Then Gideon said to God, 'Let not Your anger burn against me; let me speak just once more. Please let me test just once more with the fleece. Please let it be dry on the fleece only, and on all the ground let there be dew.' And God did so that night…" Judg. 6:36-40

My child, are you hesitating regarding something that I have clearly told you to do.

What is that thing, My child? What act of obedience and trust have I required of you? What step have I asked you to take?

Do you still, after all the many times I have shown Myself faithful on your behalf, need *proof* that I will go before you in this thing to which I have called you?

Do not doubt; do not shrink back. Step out in My Name and obey, and rely on My supply of power to enable you to accomplish the task…rely on My faithfulness to bring it to pass.

Oh My dear, precious child…

How deep is the depth of My love for you this morning! Will you let it embrace you? How high and how wide this great love, which over flows My heart toward you. Will you receive it?

My love is not dependent upon who you are or what you've done. My love for you, My child, is based upon who I am—a loving, merciful, compassionate God and Father—and upon what I've done for you—sent My beloved Son to die in your place, taking your sin and the punishment for it upon Himself so that, being completely cleansed from all your sin by His blood, you could now come and receive the love that I freely pour out upon you.

Come now, and receive of My love for you. Drink it in, My child, for I lavishly pour it out for you!

"The Lord is merciful and gracious, slow to anger and abounding instead fast love." Ps. 103:8

"Therefore you too now have sorrow; but I will see you again, and your heart will rejoice, and no one takes your joy away from you." John 16:22 (NAS 1977)

Yes, My child…no one can take that joy from you. Yet you find yourself this morning **lacking** joy.

So, to what have you **willingly sacrificed** your joy…to anxiety and worry, to the cares of this world, to the trials of life, to anger or other sin in your heart that you have allowed to snuff it out?

Remember that My Son endured the cross "for the joy set before Him." Will you also, once again, fix your eyes on the hope of heaven…the hope of being forever with the Lover of your soul…no sorrow…no sickness…no pain…no tears?

In My presence is **fullness** of joy.

At My right hand are pleasures forever. Remember this, and let joy rise in your heart again this day.

"These things I have spoken to you, that My joy may be in you, and that your joy may be full"! John 15: 11

"But I stand silently before the Lord, waiting for Him to rescue me. For salvation comes from Him alone. Yes, He alone is my rock, my rescuer, defense and fortress—why then should I be tense with fear when troubles come?
My protection and success come from God alone. He is my refuge, a rock where no enemy can reach me. O people, trust Him all the time. Pour out your longings before Him, for He can help!" Ps. 62:5-8 (TLB)

My child, continue to trust in Me—hope in Me. At times you feel as though you face your trials alone—but you do not.

I say to you, look down for a moment and see—My hand is in your own. My child, you are not alone in this, for I am holding you. I will never let go of My grip—I will not let you go!

Now look up, and see the smile of your Father, for I have seen your perseverance through the dark night and how your faith has held fast and how you desire to walk through this in a way that glorifies Me. Thank you, My child, for seeking to honor Me even in the hard times.

Stand firm, and hold fast to the Hand that holds you, and feel My great pleasure in you this morning.

"Draw near to God, and He will draw near to you." Jas. 4:8

My child, once you were far from Me, your heart completely given over to your sins and to the lust of your flesh.

But now that you are My child, why do you still shrink back and cower before Me? For I have declared you righteous, as if you had never sinned; My Son's precious blood has washed you clean.

Therefore, this morning I urge you, do not shrink back before Me, but rather step forward with confidence and the full assurance of faith to the throne of grace,

"Though your sins are as scarlet, they will be as white as snow!" Isa. 1:18b (NAS)

"…be strong in the Lord, and in the strength of His might."
Eph. 6:10
"He gives strength to the weary, and to him who lacks might He increases power." Isa. 40:29 (NAS)

Child, you feel weak this morning, and so you are—in *yourself*. But you don't need to remain in that state. All the strength and might that you need to overcome and conquer your sin can be found in Me.

Those who wait upon Me, those who linger in My empowering presence, those who *hope* in Me, *they will* renew their strength; *they will* mount up on *wings like eagles. They will* run and *not* grow weary; *they will* walk and *not* grow faint.

Come to the source of all refreshing this morning. I will strengthen you; surely, I will help you.

"Leaving the crowd, they [the disciples] too Him along with them in the boat…And there arose a fierce gale of wind, and the waves were breaking over the boat so much that the boat was already filling up.
And Jesus Himself was in the stern, asleep on the cushion; and they awoke Him and said, 'Master, Master, we are perishing, and do you not care?!'
And being aroused, He rebuked the wind and said to the sea, 'Hush, be still.' And the wind died down and it became perfectly calm." Mark 4:36-39 (NAS)

My dear one whom I love so deeply, do not be afraid this morning. For I have seen your pain. I see your fear as you watch the wind and the waves grow stronger and higher. You fear you will perish and drown.

But I tell you this morning, let faith rise up in your heart! Instead of focusing on the fierce storms that have risen around you, *remember* **Who** it is that is beside you in the boat. Am I not the One who *calms* the wind and the waves!

Fix your eyes upon Me. Call upon Me in your distress, and I will deliver you. Hope in Me for this day and for all your tomorrows!

"Rest in the Lord and wait patiently for Him." Psalm 37:7 (NAS)

Are you striving this morning, My child? Perhaps striving to earn My approval or favor instead of living in the good of it as something **I** accomplished **for** you on the cross?

Or perhaps you are striving in your work for Me? But I call you this morning to rest in My presence.

This is not a rest from doing that which I have clearly called you to do but rather a rest from striving to accomplish **God's work** in **your own strength.**

You are busy doing and running here and there, but you are running sometimes in the wrong direction and after the wrong things. Stop your running; stop your busyness and your racing mind; stop trying to **earn** My favor. Just **'be'** in the presence of a God who loves you without condition, and be refreshed, invigorated, and re-envisioned.

Then you will run, but with renewed strength, and you will be running after the things that delight **My** heart and bring **you** lasting joy.

I have many wonderful things in store for you this year, and most of them will be realized as you linger in My presence.

"Since then we have a great High Priest who has passed through the heavens, Jesus the Son of God, let us hold fast our confession.
For we do not have a high priest who cannot sympathize with our weaknesses, but one who has been tempted in all things as we are, yet without sin.
Let us therefore draw near with confidence to the throne of grace, that we may receive mercy and may find grace to help in time of need." Heb. 4:14-16 (NAS 1977)

I know your weaknesses, My beloved. I, too, was tempted in every way that you find yourself struggling,…but where you fall short, I have been victorious.

I, too, was tempted to ungodly anger, but I did not give in to it or let it have its way with Me…rather I forgave those who betrayed and tortured Me.

I was tempted by the lusts of the flesh, yet I kept My heart and My mind pure, not giving in to them or indulging in their pleasures.

I was tempted to despair as I hung there on the cross abandoned, forsaken, and in utter agony, yet for the hope that was before Me I chose to endure the cross and its shame for your sake.

This morning, will you let Me lead you to that same cross, the cross where all your sin was dealt one final blow?

This morning, will you come to the empty tomb and rejoice, knowing that My resurrection power is more than enough to give you the strength you need to help you in your weakness? More than enough!!!

"For I am convinced that neither death, nor life, nor angels, nor principalities, nor things present, nor things to come, nor powers, nor height, nor depth, nor any other created thing, shall be able to separate us from the love of God, which is in Christ Jesus our Lord." Rom. 8:38-39 (NAS)

This morning, there are those whose hearts are breaking. You see so many around you celebrating love and enjoying relationships, yet you feel lonely, and your heart yearns and cries out for love.

But beloved, I would comfort you with these words this morning:

My child, I have seen your pain and the aching of your heart. I have heard your cry and seen your tears.

But child, I want you to know that no love on earth can satisfy that longing of your heart. *Only My love for you—My perfect love*—can fulfill your every longing. And I desire to touch your heart this morning with My tender love and overwhelm you with My sweet embrace.

You are loved, My child, and loved deeply. You are loved by *Me!*

I say you are precious and beloved, holy and treasured…set apart unto Me to be used for noble purposes…

But you say, "No! I am a vessel filled with cracks, damaged and unfit for use by a King. I have been broken and spilled out and am empty. I have nothing to give."

But I say to you that you are the vessel of **My** choosing. And whom I have **called** and **chosen**, I will **enable**. Though you are broken, I will heal you. Though you are empty and have nothing to give in and of yourself, **I** have **much** that **I** desire to give **through** you. I will fill you up with My Spirit so that you will pour forth in abundance and overflow.

Place your empty, cracked vessel in My hands this morning, and watch the mighty work I will do with your life.

"Let the Word of Christ richly dwell within you." Col. 3:16
(NAS)

My children, by My Word the heavens were made. By the Word of My mouth the planets and stars were created and set in place. By the power of My Word every created thing was formed, right down to the very cell, to its own unique genetic makeup, to the very tiniest molecule.

Yet the most amazing thing is that this same almighty Word of God dwells within you who are Mine.

As you *nurture* it, it will grow within you and will *nourish* you. As you *feast* upon it, it will *satisfy* your every longing. As you *dwell* upon it, My Word will wash over you and renew your mind. As you discover and unearth its deepest, most precious treasures, it will *set you free!*

Does My Word, My powerful and creative Word, dwell in you *richly?* Are you nurturing it, feasting upon it, memorizing precious nuggets of its truth, unearthing its abundant treasures?

I say to you again this morning…let the Word of Christ *richly* dwell within you!

"Where can I go from Thy Spirit? Or where can I flee from Thy Presence? If I ascend to heaven, Thou art there; If I make my bed in Sheol, behold, Thou art there. If I take the wings of the dawn, if I dwell in the remotest part of the sea, even there Thy hand will lead me, and Thy right hand will lay hold of Me. If I say, 'Surely the darkness will overwhelm me, and the light around me will be night,' even the darkness is not dark to Thee, and the night is as bright as the day. Darkness and light are alike to Thee." Ps. 139:7-12

There are some this morning who feel as if you've entered into a black hole or a dark tunnel. You can't seem to find a way out, and you feel alone, abandoned, and desperate.

I would say to you:

I *am here*, child…you are *not* alone. Do not go by your feelings, for they will deceive you.

Stand firm on the promises of My Word—I will *never* leave you or forsake you!

"You shall therefore impress these words of Mine on your heart and on your soul; and you shall bind them as a sign on your hand, and as bands on your forehead. And you shall teach them to your sons, talking of them when you sit in your house and when you walk along the road, when you lie down and when you rise up. And you shall write [these words of Mine] on the doorposts of your house and on your gates." Deut. 11:18-20 (NAS)

M y child, fill your mind with My truth. Let the life-bringing waters of My Word seep into the dry ground of your spirit.

My words will comfort you in your trials, will strengthen you when you fall, will encourage you when you fail, will uphold you when you grow weary, will bring you peace when your heart is filled with anxiety and fear.

My words of life will sow fertile seed into your spirit that can grow and bring forth much fruit in the places where you have become stagnant.

"Let the Word of Christ dwell in you richly…"! Col. 3:16

My child, are you more aware as you stand before Me this morning of your sins, or of My *forgiveness* of your sins?

Are you more aware of your failures and mistakes, or of the blood of My Son, which *covers* them all and washes you clean of them?

Remember, My sons and daughters, remember who I am—for I am your *Father*, not a harsh or temperamental God you must appease. I have not dealt with you as you deserve. Instead of My wrath, I've poured out My love upon you.

Instead of harshness, I've shown you tenderness, compassion, and kindness…instead of judgement, I have lavished on you mercy and grace.

I am the Almighty God, but to you I am also your tender-hearted Father, and you stand before Me this morning completely forgiven. Remember this!

"O God, You are my God; early will I seek you. My soul thirsts for You, my flesh longs for You in a dry and thirsty land where no water is; to see Your power and Your glory, even as I have seen You in the sanctuary." Ps. 63:1-2 (NKJV)

My child, does your soul thirst for Me, your flesh *long* for Me? Are you in that dry and thirsty land right now, that land where there is no water?

Come to Me, for I am the Water of Life, and I will pour forth of Myself upon all your dry places and make them fertile valleys. As the woman at the well came thirsty but left satisfied, so you, too, come now, and drink freely.

And as often as you come here, I will fill you to overflowing, until your empty vessel is spilling out over the sides because it can't contain My abundance—I will not give you just enough to get by but will *saturate* you with My goodness and faithfulness, will *immerse* you in the depths of My grace, and will pour out a *deluge* upon you of My Spirit until you are *drenched!*

"The steps of a man are established by the Lord, and He delights in his way.
When he falls he will not be hurled headlong, because the Lord is the One who holds his hand." Ps. 37:23-24 (NAS)

There are some this morning who would feel that, while this verse may apply to everyone else around them, they just can't see Me guiding them and intimately involved in their lives.

But I would say to you:

You are the object of My delight. Are you aware of your hand in Mine? I *will not* let go but will guide you safely through. As a father holds his child's hand where there is danger or to help guide him in the darkness or when the way he should go is unclear, so, My child, do I have *your* hand held tightly in *My* grip. You *will not* be hurled headlong, for My hold on you is sure.

So do not fear the darkness, and do not fear because the way is not known to you. For *I know* your steps…they are *ordered* by Me, and I will safely guide you in the path I've chosen.

Oh, My child, if you only knew how often you are on My mind. Night and day you are before Me. You could not even begin to count My many precious thoughts of you, so vast is the sum of them. There is never a moment that My gaze doesn't rest upon you, My beloved.

And oh, the joy that floods My heart when you return that gaze and our eyes meet as we share sweet communion together and drink deeply of the cup of fellowship. It delights My heart at those times to pour out upon you My rich, satisfying presence and the thirst-quenching refreshment of My Spirit.

Come and dine; come and feast at My table of sweet communion, and you will be satisfied. Your peace and joy will be renewed, your hope restored, and you will not be in want for any good thing.

Remember, child, My eyes are forever upon You!

"The Lord your God is in your midst, a victorious Warrior. He will exult over you with joy, He will be quiet in His love, He will rejoice over you with shouts of joy." Zeph. 3:17 (NAS)

My beloved, I delight in you. There is no end to My love for you, nothing to compare to the pleasure I have spending quiet time with you. But I would ask this morning one question: Do you, My dear one, delight in Me? Or has spending time with Me become a duty? Do you *live* to spend these tender moments together with Me, or are you simply trying to get this 'chore' done and checked off your daily list so that you can move on to the rest of your day and to things you deem 'more *important*' and *'pressing'*.

I want you, My love, to find the great joy in Me that I find in you. I want you to long for Me, to crave our times together, to steal away with Me often during opportune moments each day just to whisper an 'I love you' and allow Me to speak to your heart of My undying love for you. I want the sparkle in your eyes to be evidence to all of our love for one another and of your delight in Me.

Delight in Me…

"For all have sinned and fall short of the glory of God, and are justified [washed totally clean] by His grace as a gift, through the redemption that is in Christ Jesus." Rom. 3:23-24

Picture with Me this morning a woman who received a precious gift made of solid silver. She was overjoyed at the gift, knowing the great price the giver had paid for it and the deep love reflected in the giving of it. She brought the priceless item out often to show its glory to others, took great care to polish it regularly so that it never showed any signs of tarnish or decay, and even placed it prominently on display. She loved how she could see her reflection in the silver as if looking into a mirror.

But as time went on, she gradually began to take the precious gift for granted, taking less and less notice of it, forgetting to polish and care for it, and eventually moving it from its prominent place where it was on display for all to see to the bottom shelf of a storage cabinet where, behind closed doors, the dust and tarnish built up on it to the point that the woman couldn't have seen her reflection in its glory even if she had tried.

I would say to you this morning, My child, have you forgotten how precious My gift of grace was to you when you first received it and what a **great price** I paid for it with the blood of My own dear Son? You would take great care with it and were amazed as you saw your reflection in it—a reflection that was free from blemish or defect, free from any trace of sin, the reflection of one made totally clean. You used to be so excited to show it and tell all about it to all who would listen…you just couldn't help yourself!

But now, have you been taking My precious, priceless gift for granted? Have you put it away on a bottom shelf behind closed doors?

Remember…remember how amazed and in awe you were when you first received My free gift of grace. This morning I would call you to bring it out of the shadows and clean the dust and tarnish off so that you see yourself once more the way **I** see you through My grace—perfect through My Son's death, blameless and holy, just as if you had never sinned.

"See how great a love the Father has bestowed upon us, that we should be called children of God; and such we are...
Beloved, now we are the children of God, and it has not yet appeared what we shall be. But we know that, when He appears, we shall be like Him, because we shall see Him just as He is.
And everyone who has this hope fixed on Him purifies himself, just as He is pure." I John 3:1-3 (NAS)

Yes, My child, how incredibly great is My love for you that I would call you, one who was an enemy of God, My child. And you are My child, even though you still battle with the sins that seem to come so easily.

And you can't imagine the good work that I can do in your heart.

But, My child, there will come a day when you will see Me, and then that good work will be complete—for you will be like Me!

So fix your eyes in hope and anticipation of that day, and prepare and purify your heart through My Holy Spirit's power and enabling—for you will see Me face-to-face! O what joy fills My heart as I look forward to being with you...My child!

"Godliness actually is a means of great gain, when accompanied by contentment." I Tim. 6:6 (NAS)

Dear one, I would call you to still your heart this morning, and let contentment bring you peace.

You search and search for the next thing that you think will make you happy. You crave for things that cannot and will not *ever* fully or permanently satisfy: food, money, entertainment, relationships, material possessions, a bigger house…

What your heart of hearts *really* craves is *Me.* When you still your anxious heart and mind and come with complete abandon into My presence, letting go in sweet surrender of everything that you have sought after to bring you fulfillment, and you linger here, you will find true refreshment, you will find that your cravings for all those other things will fade and cease, for the sweetness of being in My presence will bring you the satisfaction that you so long for.

You don't need anything else…I am *enough.* Come and let Me satisfy your soul with the joy and peace of true contentment. Let Me satisfy you with Myself.

"These things I have spoken to you, that in Me you may have peace. In the world you will have tribulation [trouble], but take courage; for I have overcome the world." John 16:33 (NAS)

My child, why do you look anxiously around you, wondering why I have deserted and abandoned you because you are now experiencing pain or hardship?

Dear one, I didn't promise you a life without tribulation. But I did say, I *will never leave you or forsake you.*

I never said your life would be one of ease, without trial or hardship. But I *did* say I would uphold you with My righteous right hand and walk close by your side through each and every one.

I did not say your life would be free of sorrow, tears, and pain. But I *did* say that I would wrap My arms of comfort around you and that I would wipe away every precious tear from your eyes.

These things I have spoken to you so that *in* your trial, in the very *midst* of your suffering and pain, you can rest in the peace that I give, you can receive comfort from Me in the tender arms of My compassionate embrace—comfort that no other can give, can know My sweet love for you in an even deeper way, and so that you will gain new courage and strength from Me to walk through to the other side.

"If You, Lord, kept a record of sins, Lord, who could stand? But with You there is forgiveness, so that we can, with reverence, serve You." Ps. 130:3-4 (NIV)

"I've fallen too far for the Lord to redeem me," you say. "His forgiveness can't possibly cover my sin."

My child, look and see: the pathway to heaven is littered with saints such as yourself who have failed miserably. Even the saints of old about whom you read in My word have given you a multitude of examples of this.

David, a man after My own heart, committed adultery, then murdered the woman's husband to hide his sin. Peter, a pillar upon which the early church was built, and My dear friend, denied three times that he even knew Me in the hour in which I needed him the most. And the list goes on and on.

But for each example of a failed saint, there is shining so brightly against that black backdrop the brilliant glory of My abundant forgiveness and grace. As a diamond radiating beauty from every facet stands out infinitely more against a dark cloth, so My grace is magnified all the more as it stands in the forefront of your shortcomings and failures.

"Consider it pure joy, my brothers and sisters, whenever you face trials of many kinds..." Jas. 1:2 (NIV)

You are weary of the battle, My child; exhausted by the many things that seem to be afflicting you, tired of constantly fighting against the things that assail you.

But dear one, your trials are opportunities for you to watch Me at work in your life; to see Me intervene on your behalf; to see yet again a visual, tangible expression of My love for you; to stand in amazement, yet again, at My power to help and deliver.

Have I not promised to work *all* things for the good of those who love Me, even those things Satan has brought upon your life in order to try to destroy you and your faith?

These triumphs are treasures that I want you to write down and pass along to the next generation after you to increase and strengthen their faith, so that they may run with boldness and resolve!

"...but just as it is written, 'Things which eye has not seen and ear has not heard, and which have not entered the heart of man, all that God has prepared for those who love Him.'" I Cor. 2:9 (NAS)

Beloved, I will lead you in a path you do not know—in a way you had not foreseen. I will perform this. It is nothing you need to create, nothing you need to contrive. No, you just simply be a willing, yielded vessel and walk in the path as I lay it out before you, following Me one step at a time as I reveal each one.

Be alert and ready, so that you are prepared, just as a soldier deployed for battle has been training hard for the days and months prior.

As a skilled warrior equips himself, be in My word often; align yourself with it. Then you will surely shoot straight, and your aim will be steady and effective. You will hit the mark that I designed and fashioned you for, the purpose for which you were created.

Lord, I desire to have the all-consuming passion back that I once had, the joy that once bubbled up out of my heart restored, the fire that burned so brightly rekindled. Help me find the way— bring me back to you.

Help me once again to hear Your voice so clearly resound in my heart with Your precious words of truth that break the chains of my guilt and sin and set this captive heart free once again.

Shake me to wake me out of my indifference and to set me back upon a fruitful path, doing Your will with all joy.

Woo me back with Your tender voice, speaking kindly to me as Your beloved. Draw me into your sweet presence where I can rest. Would you have this rebel back?

My child, I love you—I really, really love you. As you come to know My love in a deeper, fuller way, it will drive out the fear that is holding captive your heart—fear of being rejected, fear of failing… For in the presence of My love, fear cannot stand, but only joy, peace, and rest remain; for My perfect love casts out all fear.

Come to Me, and let Me show you how deep My love is for you. Yes, it is firm and steadfast, unchanging and constant. Let My love shine brightly into every area of your heart as a bright light which dispels the darkness there.

Oh My child, My precious child, I never turned away from you—I never left you. You allowed your mind to become overrun and distracted by other things, and where your mind dwells, your heart is sure to follow. In your self-sufficiency and pride, you thought you could live life independently of Me. But, I was always here—waiting, longing, anxious to be with you and to have sweet fellowship with you once again.

Do you know that these moments with you are a treasure to Me—more than many costly jewels?

Come here often and rest your spirit and refresh your soul—it will bring life to your bones, hope to your heart, and renewed vision.

Be at peace, My child, and never fear that I would ever abandon you or not take you back—My love for you is still the same. It will never change!

"How blessed are the people who know the joyful sound! Oh Lord, they walk in the light of Thy countenance. In Thy name they rejoice all the day, and by Thy righteousness they are exalted." Ps. 89:15-16 (NAS)

My child, this is a glorious new day. I have much for you in this day—even in this year—much to do **in** you, and much for you to do for Me.

I am calling you to focus on staying close to Me and then watch and see how I gradually conform you more and more into My image and change your heart.

I am calling you to focus on staying close to Me and then to watch and see how, as a natural overflow, there will pour out of you good works as gifts to others.

And it won't even seem like effort on your part, for My Spirit will do the work **in** you— and then **through** you—pouring forth from you as a river to bless, to heal, to bind up the broken-hearted, to speak My words of comfort and cheer to those who are hurting or downcast, to nourish, to strengthen, to envision.

Even your physical labors done in My Name will be fueled by the power and energy of My Spirit. At times, you won't even be consciously aware that you are doing My work, because it will just be a natural outflowing of being with Me, of living a life in My presence.

Child, stay close to Me!

"If you keep My commandments, you will abide in My love, just as I have kept My Father's commandments and abide in His love. These things I have spoken to you that My joy may be in you, and that your joy may be full." John 15:10-11

My child, do you desire the abundant joy that I am offering you? Perhaps you even sing songs that speak of this joy, but do you find that you are not walking in the good of it?

Is your joy rooted in shallow soil so that it is easily shaken when trials come or when things trouble your heart? Does your joy quickly flee away when things aren't going your way?

My child, make sure that your joy is deeply rooted in the promises of My word. Then it will be a joy unshakable. Let your heart be filled with joy that your name is written in My book of life. Rejoice in the grace that put your name there. Rejoice in the blood that poured forth at the cross to wash you whiter than snow.

Yes, lift up your countenance this day. Let joy fill your heart and a smile broaden on your face as you sense My smile toward you. For when I look at you, I see My beloved Son, and what joy and delight that brings to *My* heart!

Be ***filled with joy*** this day!

"Behold the former things have come to pass; now I declare new things. Before they spring forth I proclaim them to you." Isa. 42:9 (NAS)

Some this morning are carrying with them the baggage of their past and trying to bear up under heavy burdens.

But I would say to you:

I died not only to forgive your sins, but also to bear your burdens, to free you from crippling guilt, to redeem your pain and heal the scars you bear, to comfort your sorrows.

Come this morning as you are…just as you are…come to the cross. Bring your burdens with you, and let Me lift them from you.

Bring the broken pieces of your heart, and let Me bind up your wounds.

"Come to Me all you who are weary and heavy-laden and I will give you rest. Take My yoke upon you and learn from Me, for I am gentle and humble in heart and you will find rest for your souls. For My yoke is easy and My burden is light." Matt. 11:28 (NAS)

"'Come now, and let us reason together,' says the Lord. 'Though your sins are as scarlet, they will be as white as snow.'" Isa. 1:18 (NAS)

Whiter than snow…whiter than snow, My child! As the beauty and purity of a freshly fallen snow, so there is now *no* stain upon *you*. Your sins *are no more.*

At the foot of the cross, all things are made *new*. Beneath the cleansing flow of My blood are all things washed clean.

Are you living in the *good* of this? Are you filled with the *joy* of this?…that though your sins were as scarlet, behold, now they are white as snow!

There are some this morning who are very aware of their thirst, and those who are very aware of the dry, desert place that their souls are in right now. I would encourage you with this passage:

"But now hear, O Jacob My servant, Israel whom I have chosen! Thus says the Lord who made you, who formed you from the womb and will help you: Fear not, O Jacob My servant, Jeshurun whom I have chosen. For I will pour water on the thirsty land, and streams on the dry ground." Isa. 44:1-3a

My child, you thirst. But are you aware that it is the very grace of God that you are aware of that thirst?! And though your soul be dry and barren, is it not I who have revealed this truth to you and helped you to see your lack?

My child, take heart! For this is an evidence of My Spirit working in your life that you are even aware of your thirst and dryness! And you can trust my word, which is truth and shall not return void, that *I will* pour water on your thirsty land and streams on your dry ground!

"If we are faithless, He remains faithful—for He cannot deny Himself." II Tim. 2:13

Dear one, My love for you does not change when you are negligent of Me. Though it saddens My heart greatly when you don't fellowship with Me, I love you none the less.

I will always remain faithful to you, because that is *Who I am.* And you will always remain My dearly beloved child, for that is who *you* are to *Me.*

Your self-sufficiency and willful independence grieve Me, but they make you *no less Mine!*

For My love for you is not about you—whether or not you behave as you should or do the things you ought. My love for you is all about **Me**—My father's heart to love even the wayward, unruly, prodigal child and bring him back home, not because he is worthy in and of himself, but because *he is My son* and I *love* him.

Child, you are Mine, and I love you forever and always. Will you come home to Me this morning?

My child, My hand is upon you. I will continue to care for you, nurture you, and help you to grow as you seek Me with all of your heart.

For I have called you by your name, and I make *no mistakes,* My child. I have called you to serve Me in ways that no other can. I will prepare you for them. Simply be open to My Spirit and His leadings.

My will most certainly will be accomplished in your life—know that—rest in that. Trust in Me, the Good Shepherd who leads His sheep into green pastures. Walk in My ways, and I will not disappoint you.

How precious you are to Me, My child. And would I let you go now? My love toward you is unchanging and faithful. I will *never* let you go. Find peace and rest in this.

"Hope deferred makes the heart sick." Prov. 13:12

M y child, you feel weak this morning. But it is because you have lost your vision. You have forgotten where your hope lies, you have become swallowed up by cares, and your heart is sick.

But I would remind you, My child, that all the hope that you need is in Me. Remember and cling to the hope of the Gospel, the hope of salvation and forgiveness of sin, the hope that I have washed you pure and clean through My sacrifice on the cross.

Then, just walk out your door and look around you. Everywhere you go, there are people living without hope…there are people dying without hope…people who **desperately need** to hear that I love them and that I died to save them and give them an abundant, hope-filled life!

Will you receive My hope and embrace it anew this morning so that you can receive strength and go out from this place bringing the gift of hope—My hope—to a world that has none?

"…but just as it is written, 'Things which eye has not seen and ear has not heard, and which have not entered the heart of man, all that God has prepared for those who love Him.'" I Cor. 2:9 (NAS)

Such wonderful things I have planned for you…will you believe this? Are you living today filled with the hope of heaven? Or, even though you believe in this wonderful place I have prepared for you, are you living more for the here and now?

Amazing and wondrous things I have prepared for <u>you</u>…will you allow this truth to reassure your heart before Me?

There is a <u>good path</u> that I have laid before you, and at the end of that path the beginning of things far too glorious for you to fathom, too wonderful for you to comprehend!

And above all, I am there, to receive you with great joy unto Myself. Oh, My child, if you only knew what awaits you!

Let the glory of heaven and the hope that fills you of spending forever there with the lover of your soul spur you on to run each and every day hard and focused after Me, filled with the great expectation of <u>that</u> day!

"...I have called you friends, for all that I have heard from My Father I have made known to you. You did not choose Me, but I chose you..." John 15:15b-16a

My child, I have called *you* My friend. Even when you were unaware, I have been your faithful companion through all the years.

You have said in your heart many times, "No one who *really* ever knew me could ever truly *love* me."

But I am the One who knows you the *best*, and yet loves you the *most*, more than any other ever has, does, or will. Even when you were unaware of My presence, I have always been with you, always been by your side, never left you...never will.

I knew all your days, all your shortcomings, all your past, present and future sins, all your failures. I knew them all *before* I chose you and called you to be My child. I knew I was getting a pot filled with cracks and chips, but I knew that I would fill *that* pot with *My* glory. *I* am the *treasure* within your pot of clay.

And know this...that I *will be* with you, your closest friend, no matter what you *do*, or *don't do*. No matter what you face tomorrow—I will be there. No matter what the next year holds—I will be by your side then, too—helping, upholding, comforting, strengthening, equipping, providing, and carrying burdens too heavy for you to bear...loving you!

I *know* you best, and I have called you My *friend*...*forever*...because of My blood shed for you!

"So it came about when Moses held his hands up, that Israel prevailed...But Moses' hands were heavy. Then they took a stone and put it under him, and he sat on it; and Aaron and Hur supported his hands, one on one side and one on the other. Thus his hands were steady until the sun set." Exod. 17:11-12 (NAS)

My child, although your own personal battle rages, I am the One holding up your arms! You are weak, but I am your strength. You are afraid that your trials will overtake and swallow you up in defeat as an enemy that seeks your destruction. But do not fear...for I will turn the tide of the battle as you lift your hands to Me.

Raise your arms in praise, remembering My goodness and faithfulness, remembering My promises, remembering My great might demonstrated over and over again in your life and the lives of so many others, remembering My undying love for you.

Despite the fact that the troubles in your life are severe and unrelenting, My power will ride forth on the wings of your praises, and I will give you the victory.

"But now thus says the Lord, He who created you, O Jacob, he who formed you, O Israel: 'Fear not, for I have redeemed you; I have called you by name, you are mine. When you pass through the waters, I will be with you; and through the rivers, they shall not overwhelm you; When you walk through fire you shall not be burned, and the flame shall not consume you. For I am the Lord your God, the Holy One of Israel, your Savior.'"
Isa. 43:1-3a

D o not worry, My child…do not fear…for I am with you wherever you go! I will go before you and make a way through the waters that you cannot see as of yet.

Press into Me; press into My word, not only so that you may be able to stand strong against the doubts that come and the storms that assail you but also so that you can link arms with others around you that are struggling and you can support, encourage, and strengthen them with the strength that you have received.

Cast all your cares upon Me, for I care for you…and help your brothers and sisters who are hurting and afraid to do the same.

My Masterpiece

"I will instruct you and teach you in the way you should go; I will counsel you with My eye upon you." Ps. 32:8

My child, I love you. My hand is upon your life. You cannot see the end from the beginning, but I, the One who directs your steps...I can. You cannot see the way before you now, as the road seems dark and bleak. But I see all things clearly, and I am upholding you with My right arm and guiding you on the pathway of righteousness. You cannot see the finished work that I am creating with your life, but I can see the beautiful, strong tapestry I am weaving. Rest in the hands of the Craftsman, and know that I am the Weaver and not you yourself.

Know that no stitch in the fabric of your life is a mistake, but is the careful design of My hands.

And I will look upon My handiwork, My masterpiece, and say, This is very good...a testimony to the faithful working of My hands and a glory to My Name!

"I cried to Him with my mouth, and He was [highly praised] with my tongue. If I regard wickedness in my heart the Lord will not hear. But certainly God has heard; He has given heed to the voice of my prayer. Blessed be God, who has not turned away my prayer, nor His lovingkindness from me." Ps. 66:17-20 (NAS)

I have heard, My child...I have heard.

The desperate cries of your heart in the darkness of the night have not fallen to the floor. Nor have they fallen on deaf ears or to a god who is indifferent, uncaring, weak, or powerless to deliver.

They have risen before My very throne, the throne of your heavenly Father who loves you dearly, the Almighty God who not only cares about you deeply but is also **all-powerful**, able to effect changes that seem completely impossible to you right now, able to deliver beyond what you can even imagine.

Certainly I have heard your cry... Trust, My precious child, in My lovingkindness toward you and in My unlimited power to deliver and save!

"Come and see the works of God, Who is awesome in His deeds toward the sons of men." Ps. 66:5 (NAS)

Legacy of Love

My child, I died for your sins at a point when you hated Me. Would I now withdraw that love that I so willingly shed for you?

How much more, now that you are My precious child, beloved to Me, will I not quickly come when you call and wrap My loving arms around you, drawing you close to Me, pulling your head to My chest...Look at the nail scars in these hands that hold you, and remember the legacy of My love for you.

My love for you did not originate with you, nor is it dependent upon you...It is truly love you don't deserve but love that I freely poured out upon the cross.

And how much more so will I now continue to pour out My love upon My children!

Look at the nail scars in these hands that hold you, and remember the legacy of My love for you...remember...

"The Lord redeems the soul of His servants; And none of those who take refuge in Him will be condemned." Ps. 34:22 (NAS)

Have you forgotten? You are redeemed! I have set you free!

You are no longer a slave to sin, and you are no longer sentenced to condemnation and death **because** of your sin…no longer to be held guilty and face the punishment you deserve.

You are righteous now, cleansed with My blood. O rejoice, My child, rejoice this morning… for though your sins were as scarlet, now you are whiter than snow!

Breathe in deeply of this truth, and let it set you free!

"I am the Lord. I have called you in righteousness. I will also hold you by the hand and watch over you. And I will appoint you as a covenant to the people, as a light to the nations, to open blind eyes; to bring out prisoners from the dungeon, and those who dwell in darkness from the prison." Isa. 42:6-7 (NAS)

Picture a man walking into the depths of a dark tunnel. It is utter darkness. Then the man lights the torch he is carrying. Although the tunnel is dark, those inside can now see because of the light which the man brought to them.

I would say this morning:

My child, I lay before you a challenge, a commission, and a calling this day. I am calling you to go out from this place into the depths of the darkness of this world. I am the Light of the world, and I **dwell** in **you**. As you shine forth My glory in the darkness, I will be able to use you to give sight to those who now cannot see My amazing grace.

Satan has held captive many souls. But I am sending you to set them free. I have given you the key, My glorious Gospel, to unlock their cell doors and loosen their shackles, to remove the chains that bind them. I have set **you** free from **your** chains; now I am sending you this day to go free others!

"Open up, ancient gates! Open up, ancient doors, and let the King of glory enter. Who is the King of glory? The LORD of Heaven's Armies— He is the King of glory." Ps. 24:9-10 (NLT)

Yes, My children, open up the gates of your hearts to Me now, that the King of Glory may come in! And lift up your voices and cry out to Me now, for I am the Lord, strong and mighty, strong to deliver, mighty to save. I am the Lord of Hosts! Is the problem that you face too large for Me to overcome? Is your foe too mighty for Me to conquer?

I say again, open your hearts, and I will come in...cry out to Me, and I will hear and answer, "for the eyes of the Lord move to and fro throughout the earth that [I] may <u>strongly support</u> those whose heart is completely [Mine]" (II Chr. 16:9)." (NAS)

"God is our refuge and strength, a very present help in trouble. Therefore we will not fear though the earth gives way, though the mountains be moved into the heart of the sea, though its waters roar and foam, though the mountains tremble at its swelling... There is a river whose streams make glad the city of God...The Lord of hosts is with us; the God of Jacob is our fortress." Ps. 46:1-4a, 7

Although these are troubling times, My child, do not fear or be anxious, for I am your refuge, your strength, your provision. I am not somewhere afar off watching with indifference.

No, I am near, a very present help in this time of trouble...I am very present with you, My precious child.

No matter what nations make an uproar or totter, no matter what changes, what slips, what roars, foams, or quakes...I am in the midst of you, and you will not be moved.

I will help you. I am with you, and I am your stronghold. And even when you face various troubles, My streams will make your heart glad as you trust in Me.

In I Kings 18, Elijah the prophet had a great victory. When he prayed, God sent down fire from heaven; then God helped him to defeat all the false prophets of Baal.

In chapter 19, he is on the run for his life, flees to the wilderness, flops down under a juniper tree, and tells God he wants to die.

Verse 19:5 says, "He lay down and slept under a juniper tree; and behold, there was an angel touching him, and he said to him, 'Arise, eat. God has provided bread because the journey is too great for you.'" (NAS) There was a cake baked on hot stones and a jar of water. The Lord provided twice in this way. Elijah arose and ate and drank, and Scripture says he "went in the strength of that food forty days and forty nights to Horeb, the mountain of God."

I would encourage some this morning:

You have won great victories, but now you feel hopeless. You are on the verge of giving up. Your strength is gone, and you feel like the journey is too great for you.

But do not be discouraged, My child; neither be afraid for your life, for I, the Lord you God, am with You, and I am mighty to save.

Arise and eat, for I have provided abundantly for all your needs. You will have no lack, for I am a good Father and a faithful provider, and I will strengthen you and bring you safely to My holy mountain.

"Moses didn't realize as he came back down the mountain with the tablets that his face glowed from being in the presence of God." Exod. 34:29 (TLB)

My child, can people tell when you have been with Me? Can they see the evidence of it in your countenance or because they see My peace and joy shining through you?

Just as the moon reflects the light and glory of the sun, even so you, too, reflect My glory and light to a world darkened by sin and despair.

Show them what I look like by living for Me. Show them My glory and light by reflecting My character and My love for them.

The more time you spend soaking in the radiant light of My presence, the more you will project that light into the dark corners of this world.

"You make known to me the path of life; in your presence there is fullness of joy; at your right hand are pleasures forevermore." Ps. 16:11

My child, what is your happiness or joy contingent upon? How would you complete the sentence, "I would be happy if only I had _____"?

Haven't I told you that nothing else will satisfy the deep longings of your heart but Me? These other things you seek are wooden idols that do not fulfill but rather leave you emptier than before.

You must find your joy, satisfaction, happiness, and contentment in Me, and only in Me. Only I can bring true and lasting joy.

Everything else is a temporary, counterfeit measure.

"You make him joyful with gladness in Your presence." Ps. 21:6b (NAS)

"The Lord is near to all who call on him, to all who call on him in truth." Ps. 145:18

My child, I am not distant or far off.

Neither am I preoccupied or distracted. No…I am near to you, and I hear every time you call to Me. I am the One who holds all things together, but I am also the One who holds your hand and hears and answers every prayer.

I know that your heart is filled with fear for your children and that they are heavy on your heart. You desire nothing more passionately than that they would receive My free gift of salvation and know Me personally—their heavenly Father—and walk with Me. You fear for them in this world in which they live, where sin is celebrated and temptations call to them from every street corner.

But I want you to entrust them to Me.

They are yours for only a little while…they are Mine for eternity, and I care as deeply about them, My precious child, as I do about you. And haven't I promised that I will not lose one of My own?

"And you shall love the Lord your God with all your heart, and with all your soul, and with all your mind, and with all your strength." Mark 12:30

Picture with Me a person shopping for the perfect gift for someone they love dearly, to bring joy and delight to their heart.

Do you love **Me?** Then let Me tell you what gift would bring Me joy and would delight **My** heart…Give Me all!

Yes, My child…I want **all** of you.

What part of your heart or life are you holding back from Me? That's the part I want the most. What are you holding back because you fear what I will do with it or what I will call you to do with it? You can trust Me with that thing, as I love you deeply and have only good for you.

Give Me all, My child…hold nothing back. Leave no room in your heart locked and off limits to Me. I want all. And when you have given all to Me, I will give you in its place something more beautiful than you could ever imagine—I will give you Myself!

A pauper was invited to a banquet with the King. The King not only invited him but also, knowing that the man had nothing but rags to wear and no appropriate attire for such an affair, gave him exquisite and beautiful robes from His own wardrobe.

However, the pauper never washed or removed any of his dirty, filthy, foul-smelling garments before putting on the beautiful items.

I believe the Lord would say:

My child, you must first put off before you can put on. You must offer up to Me your filthy garments and allow Me to cleanse you from all unrighteousness, washing you with My blood, which I poured out on the cross for you. And, in exchange for your rags, I will dress you in My robes of righteousness. Let Me clothe you in fine linen whiter than snow.

In Psalm 39:12-13, David is crying out to God in utter despair. However, in the verses that immediately follow, he begins praising God for healing him.

My child, the bruised one I will heal; the broken one I will restore. The one whose heart has been torn asunder I will repair and tenderly knit back together. The one whose life and dreams have been shattered I will piece back together stronger than before.

Why? Why would I heal one so lowly and unworthy, so underserving, you ask? To show forth My glory to the world—so that many will see and revere and will trust in the Me!

Also, to show you just how much I love you. You are precious to Me, and I care deeply about you.

So, do not despair, My child, for I will restore you!

My child, you've been struggling, you've been fighting, you've been wrestling with seemingly overwhelming obstacles in your life.

But this morning I am calling you to rest. I am calling you to remember that the battle belongs to Me, your Lord, and I will take up your cause. I will fight where you don't have the strength. I will give you the victory that you haven't been able to achieve in your own might.

My power **will** deliver you!

"Then Moses called Bezalel and Oholiab and every skillful person in whom the Lord had put skill, everyone whose heart stirred him, to come to the work to perform it." Exod. 36:2 (NAS)

What skills have I invested in you, My child?

What can I use that you can give to the building of My kingdom?

My child, I have given you all that you need to do what I've called you to do. I've equipped you with skills that I designated specifically for you in order for you to perform the work to which I have called you.

Is your heart stirring you this morning to come with your skills, giftings, and talents to the work to perform it? Are you ready to give back to Me for My glory and for the building of My church all that I have placed within you?

If not, what is holding you back? Find that thing and uproot it, lest the talents that you have be removed. Those skills that you reinvest into the building of My kingdom I will multiply exponentially!

"For I will set My eyes on them for good, and I will bring them again to this land; and I will build them up and not overthrow them, and I will plant them and not pluck them up. And I will give them a heart to know Me, for I am the Lord; and they will be My people, and I will be their God, for they will return to Me with their whole heart." Jer. 24:6-7 (NAS)

My child, I have heard you cry out, "God, give me more of a desire to know you! I don't desire you the way I should…help me!"

Child, this verse is in answer to your heart-felt prayer. I will give **you** a heart to know Me. This is a prayer I delight to answer! Child, do you realize that the very fact that you are even praying for this is evidence that I am at work through My Holy Spirit's power in your life?

Let this knowledge breathe hope into your heart…I who have begun a good work in you will—**most certainly**—complete it! And what a masterpiece it will be when I am through!

"But our citizenship is in heaven. And we eagerly await a Savior from there, the Lord Jesus Christ." Phil. 3:20 (NIV)
"Maranatha! [Come, O Lord!]" I Cor. 16:22b (NIV)

My child, look around you at the world I've created for your pleasure, not only for you to enjoy, but ultimately to point your attention to Me, the Author and Creator of all.

You look in wonder at something I've created, such as DNA, then you look closer still as your technological ability advances, and you marvel all the more! The diversity of the birds of the air, the uniformity and design of a single snowflake, the amazing complexity of a single cell, the masterful engineering of the human eye—all of these things point to a wonderful, creative Master Designer.

As you enjoy what I have blessed you with in this temporal world, remember how much infinitely better heaven will be. Things in this world are a dim reflection of the magnificence of My ultimate creation, and I long for the day when you will be here with Me and I can show you all of its grandeur!

But, even more than that, I long to reveal **Myself** to you, to reveal to you ALL that I am and the true majesty of the One you have been worshiping! With new eyes, you will be able to behold the true glory and splendor of your God! Let anticipation grip your heart, as it does Mine, for this sweet and wonderful reunion!

L ord, I give You **all** of me today. Please help me not to hold back **any** part of my heart or my life from You.

Help me to want **Your** will more than I want my own.

Fan the dimly burning flame in my heart into a raging fire, that I would burn for You.

Open the eyes of my spirit and my understanding.

Cause me to hunger and thirst for You, and satisfy my heart with Your goodness.

Breathe the life of Your Holy Spirit into my spirit, and cause me to **come alive** to You!

Help me to keep my heart, mind, and body pure and not to entertain perverted thoughts or to engage in impure actions.

Lift my eyes to see Your great grace, which is Your free gift of salvation to this undeserving recipient, and to see Your goodness and kindness to me, even when I deserved Your wrath and merited death for my sin.

May You cause Christ to become the greatest treasure of my heart, that I would cherish Him more than anything else this world has to offer.

Fill my heart with a desire to be with You, basking in Your presence, being refreshed and renewed by Your Holy Spirit.

Give me a love for Your word, that I would devour it as I would choice morsels at the King's banquet table. Renew my mind with Your word.

Check out other products by Wendy Anne Hunt at: WendyAnneHunt.com

Books in Print

The Orphan and the King, Volume I: **The Freedom Mission**

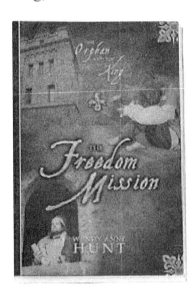

The Orphan and the King, Volume II: **Love's Great Ransom**

The Orphan and the King, Volume III: **The Final Conquest**

Let your imagination soar to a land filled with kings and wizards, dragons and damsels in distress, dungeons, dwarves, and enchanted forests. Fantasy and reality meet in a suspenseful story of love, honor, and courage against all odds...of faith and hope...magic and mystery...treachery, treason, and terror...compassion and redemption!

CD's

Promises in the Night I

Each of these CD's contains 70 minutes of comforting, encouraging, Scriptures. Children will hear God's precious promises throughout Scripture, in language they can understand, spoken in soothing tones with peaceful music and soft nature sounds for bedtime listening. As your children's bodies are renewed in sleep, let their minds be renewed by God's comforting words!

For ages 1 to 101 **(in CD and MP3 format)**

Made in the USA
Middletown, DE
28 January 2023

23253192R00216